MERC

MERC

American Soldiers of Fortune

JAY MALLIN
AND
ROBERT K. BROWN

CASEMATE

Philadelphia & Oxford

Published in the United States of America and Great Britain in 2018 by
CASEMATE PUBLISHERS
1950 Lawrence Road, Havertown, PA 19083, USA
and
The Old Music Hall, 106–108 Cowley Road, Oxford OX4 1JE, UK

Paperback Edition: ISBN 978-1-61200-591-1
Digital Edition: ISBN 978-1-61200-592-8 (epub)

A CIP record for this book is available from the British Library

Printed and bound in the United States of America

For a complete list of Casemate titles, please contact:

CASEMATE PUBLISHERS (US)
Telephone (610) 853-9131
Fax (610) 853-9146
Email: casemate@casematepublishers.com
www.casematepublishers.com

CASEMATE PUBLISHERS (UK)
Telephone (01865) 241249
Fax (01865) 794449
Email: casemate-uk@casematepublishers.co.uk
www.casematepublishers.co.uk

Contents

Acknowledgements

The material for this book was gathered from a variety of sources. A number of the mercs were personal friends or acquaintances of the authors. In some instances personal interviews were conducted by the authors. Other material came from the personal files of the authors. Books that were particularly useful included *Cast a Giant Shadow* by Ted Berkman, *The Lafayette Escadrille* by Herbert Molloy Mason, Jr., *Chennault and the Flying Tigers* by Anna Chennault, *John Paul Jones* by Samuel Eliot Morison, *Webster's American Military Biographies, George Washington and the American Revolution* by Burke Davis, *The Damned Die Hard* by Hugh McLeave, *Major Mike* by Mike Williams, and *The Encyclopedia of Military History* by R. Ernest Dupuy and Trevor N. Dupuy.

Thanks go to the staff of *Soldier of Fortune* magazine, including N. E. MacDougald, Dana Drenkowski, Robin Heid, Lou Jones, Suzanne Nielsen, Mary Jenkins, and Robert Poos.

Special thanks and credit must go to E. J. "Sandy" Hackney, who had the concept for the book and whose assistance, especially in research, was most valuable as the work progressed.

War is an ugly thing, but not the ugliest of things; the decayed and degraded state of moral and patriotic feeling which thinks that nothing is worth war is much worse.

A man who has nothing for which he is willing to fight; nothing he cares about more than his own personal safety; is a miserable creature who has no chance of being free, unless made and kept so by the exertions of better men than himself.

—JOHN STUART MILL

CHAPTER I

Who Are the Mercs?

They call themselves "mercs"—a contraction of the word "mercenaries." The very word has an unsavory connotation: mercenaries are men who fight for money. The implication is that they fight only for money; they are warm bodies for hire. Did the word "mercenary" (noun) derive from the adjective "mercenary" ("hireling; venal" says the dictionary) or vice versa? Whatever. The soldier who is a mercenary is viewed as a person who fights only for money, and presumably his other morals are equally negotiable.

It is true that many mercenaries have fought and are fighting today primarily for monetary reward. There are, however, two additional important motivations that affect mercenaries: There have been many who have gone to war because of their love of adventure and of fighting. Theodore Roosevelt described this succinctly: "All men who feel any power of joy in battle know what it is like when the wolf rises in the heart."

A third motive for mercenary activities is belief in a cause. There have been mercenaries who fought because they truly believed in the cause for which they were fighting. Outstanding examples in American history were the Marquis de Lafayette, a Frenchman who came to fight for the American colonies, and Mickey Marcus, an American who went to fight for Israeli independence.

Until the French revolution, when a nation of citizens flocked to the colors and outnumbered the small "professional" military forces each European kingdom had employed, the term "mercenary" did not carry with it a negative connotation. Military personnel of the day were employed directly by the king for money—the average citizen was perceived as not having a stake in the country to fight for.

It was the French Revolution that gave the average citizen a feeling that he had a vested interest in his nation-state. His newfound willingness to fight for his country caused him suddenly to look down his nose at those persons he saw fighting for mere cash—a seemingly baser motivation than patriotism. In fact, each embarrassed the other: the "noble" citizen who took less cash for the job the mercenary was demanding more money for, and the mercenary whose very presence in the same military forces made the citizen's cause seem a bit baser and more transient. Pragmatism, however, has forced both government and citizen to accept the concept of mercenaries, if not the word, for the duration of whatever conflict in which they find themselves.

The authors could easily fall into the trap of defending the word "mercenary," or they could use other, more colloquially acceptable terms. In fact, one man's terrorist is another man's freedom fighter. A mercenary fighting on one side becomes a "foreign volunteer" or a "military advisor," while those performing the same task on the other side become "mercenaries" or "enemies of the people" or "whores of war." The authors feel the term mercenary will outlast the various systems and groups that now ascribe to it negative connotations; it will endure through future centuries as a term describing a condition of fact, without editorial innuendo. But for the time being, mercenary is a "bad" word, even to those who employ mercenaries.

Because of the connotation of the word, it is clearly a disservice to label Lafayette and Marcus and others like them as mercenaries, because their motive for fighting was not money. Let us say, therefore, that all men who fight under foreign colors are "soldiers of fortune," and that "fortune" in that context refers as much to luck as to gold. Some soldiers of fortune fight for gold, some fight for cause, and some fight for excitement. All mercenaries are soldiers of fortune, but not all soldiers of fortune are mercenaries.

Are soldiers of fortune effective fighters? Niccòlo Machiavelli in *The Prince* provided this devastating opinion:

> Mercenaries and auxiliaries are useless and dangerous, and a leader having his state built on mercenary armies will never be secure. Troops of this sort are disunited, ambitious, undisciplined, and faithless, swaggering when among friends and cowardly in the face of the enemy; they have neither fear of God nor loyalty to men. Ruin is postponed only as long as the assault is postponed; in times of peace you are despoiled by them and in time of war by the enemy. The reason is that they have no other interest or incentive to hold the field, save only their moderate pay, which is not enough to make them willing to die for you. They are pleased to be your soldiers so long as you have no war; when it comes they either run away or leave your employ.

A totally different view was offered by the English poet Alfred E. Housman. Germany's Kaiser had sarcastically called the British army "an army of mercenaries," referring to the numerous colonial units it contained. Housman retorted with his "Epitaph on an Army of Mercenaries," as follows:

> These, in the days when heaven was falling,
> The hour when earth's foundations fled,
> Followed their mercenary calling
> And took their wages and are dead.
>
> Their shoulders held the sky suspended;
> They stood, and earth's foundations stay;
> What God abandoned, these defended,
> And saved the sum of things for pay.

This brief poem was to play a role in the creation of one of the most famous soldier of fortune units in American history. Mrs. Anna Chennault in her biography of her husband, commander of the World War II Flying Tigers—a mercenary unit —stated that Colonel Chennault felt that "one of the factors that turned the scales" in favor of allowing the formation of this unit in President Roosevelt's mind was Housman's poetic defense of mercenaries.

The history of soldiers of fortune is as old as the history of man warring on man. In Biblical times, David, an Israelite, killed Goliath, a Philistine, but later defected to the Philistines and conducted raids for them. Among the earliest mercenaries —predating even David—were the Numidian troops led by the Egyptian pharaoh, Ramses II, in his unsuccessful attempt to capture Kadesh, a Hittite stronghold, in 1294 B.C. The Persian Darius the Great utilized Greek mercenaries; the vaunted Roman legions sometimes included Balearic and Aegean mercenaries, and such great military leaders as William the Conqueror, Tamerlane, and Gustavus Adolphus had mercenaries among the men under their command. Mercenary detachments—St. Bernard of Siena called them "locusts who leap here and there"—were a part of the European military scene for centuries. To this day the popes are guarded by Swiss mercenaries, the Foreign Legion is a part of the French Army, and Indian Gurkhas serve in the British Army.

Thus, in view of the long European tradition of utilizing soldiers of fortune, it was natural that soldiers of fortune would participate on both sides when the American colonies fought to break away from England. The British first considered hiring twenty thousand Russians. A British nobleman commented that the Russians "will be charming visitors at New York and civilise that part of America wonderfully." Catherine the Great, however, rejected the British plan. So the British accepted the offer of minor German princes to rent them troops—this was a normal way for the princes to obtain revenue. A total of 29,166 Germans from six principalities would serve the British monarch in America, nearly half of them Hessians from Hesse-Cassel. Although the Germans served throughout the Revolutionary War, American history best remembers them for General Washington's bold and successful strike against the Hessian garrison at Trenton, New Jersey, on December 26, 1776.

On the side of the colonials there was, of course, the young and gallant Marquis de Lafayette, able commander and accomplished diplomat who was instrumental in securing decisive military assistance from France. There were also the Baron von Steuben, who doggedly transformed the American troops from rabble to regulars; Thomas Conway, the Irishman; Johann Kalb, German; and Tadeusz Kościuszko and Kazimierz Pulaski, Poles. All of these were soldiers of fortune; all served the American cause well.

In a little over two centuries of history since the Revolutionary War, the United States has engaged in seven major wars: against England, Mexico, Spain, Germany and its allies, Germany and Japan and their allies, North Korea and North Vietnam, and in a good many lesser military actions. In 1970 a congressional subcommittee published a list of 165 major and minor "instances of use of United States armed forces abroad, 1798–1970."

Thousands of foreign nationals have served with the U.S. armed forces over the years. Some were drafted (residents of the United States, they were subject to the same laws as American citizens). Many others, however, volunteered for service. Similarly, hundreds of Americans, possibly thousands, have served in the armies, navies, and air forces of other nations. Usually they signed up as individuals. In this century, however, there have been at least four cases of Americans fighting under foreign flags in units composed entirely or largely of Yanks. There were the Escadrille Lafayette of World War I, the Kościuszko Squadron which fought for Poland in the Russian-Polish War of 1920, the Lincoln and Washington battalions of the Spanish Civil War, and the Flying Tigers of World War II.

Since World War II, American soldiers of fortune have found their skills to be most in demand in the small wars of Africa and Latin America. They fought yesterday, they fight today, and they will continue to fight tomorrow. Some never come home; others move up to replace them. The spirit of the soldier of fortune was best expressed by a young American soldier of fortune long ago—July 3, 1915—in a letter he wrote to his mother from France. A most unlikely mercenary, Alan Seeger, Harvard man and poet, was one of the Americans who had flocked to join the Foreign Legion when France entered World War I.

Seeger wrote from the front:

"Had I the choice I would be nowhere else in the world than where I am. Even had I the chance to be liberated, I would not take it. Do not be sorrowful then. It is the shirkers and slackers alone in this war who are to be lamented. The tears for those who take part in it and who do not return should be sweetened by the sense that their death was the death which beyond all others they would have chosen for themselves, that they went to it smiling and without regret, feeling that whatever value their continued presence in the world might be to humanity, it could not be greater than the example and inspiration they were to it in so departing. We to whom the idea of death is familiar, walking always among the little mounds and crosses of the men *mort au champ d'honneur* know what this means. If I thought you could feel about me as I feel about them, the single self-reproach I have, that of causing you possible unhappiness, would be mitigated."

On July 4, 1916, Legionnaire Alan Seeger was killed in combat as the Legion attacked the enemy-held village of Belloy-en-Santerre.

There follow the accounts of eight contemporary American soldiers of fortune. Some have come back; some have not.

CHAPTER 2

William Morgan: From Intrigue to Frogs

"I was wearing a two-hundred-fifty-dollar suit, white-on-white shirt, and thirty-seven-dollar shoes. I looked like a real fat-cat tourist—but I only had four dollars in my pocket." Thus did William Morgan describe his arrival in Cuba during that nation's civil war in 1957.

Many people believe that Fidel Castro won the Cuban civil war/revolution. Fidel Castro believes it. The fact is, however, that a large number of Cubans from all walks of life participated in that struggle, and a number of these people played significant leadership roles. Castro became a symbol: he was young, charismatic, public relations–conscious, and there was a romantic aura about him. The reality, however, was that Castro was the leader of but one of several revolutionary entities engaged in the war against Dictator Fulgencio Batista.

One of the other military leaders was an American, William Alexander Morgan. If soldiers of fortune can, by the very nature of their calling, be termed "colorful," none is more aptly described by that word than Morgan. During the course of his career he was a United States soldier, a fugitive from justice, a guerrilla chieftain, the "mayor" of a Cuban city, a master international intriguer, a high-ranking officer in a foreign army—and a frog farmer.

Morgan's adventures began early in his life. He was born April 18, 1928, in Cleveland, Ohio. Although his father was, in Morgan's words, a "solid Republican," Morgan ran with the wrong crowd, "ran away from home so many times," and finally, at fifteen, ran away from school. In March, 1946, he was picked up by the San Antonio police and a month later by the Toledo police, who suspected him of armed robbery but did not book him. When he was eighteen he enlisted in the Army and after training was sent to serve with the occupation forces in Japan. He married a Japanese girl (and, being truly international, he later married an American girl in the United States and a Cuban girl in Cuba). Not very literate, fond of comic books, Morgan evidently was quite a talker: in the Army he was nicknamed "Gabby."

In November, 1947, Morgan was arrested for being AWOL and was sentenced to three months at hard labor with forfeiture of pay during that period. At the stockade in Kyoto, Japan, Morgan overpowered a guard, taking his pistol and uniform, and escaped. Recaptured and court-martialed, Morgan was found guilty of escape and armed robbery. His sentence:

> To be dishonorably discharged from the service, to forfeit all pay and allowance due or to become due, and to be confined at hard labor, at such place as the reviewing authority may direct, for five (5) years.

Morgan did his time at the federal reformatories at Chillicothe, Ohio and Milan, Michigan. He was not a model prisoner: he was placed in solitary on several occasions for fighting, attempted escape, refusal to work, and attempted arson. (One of Morgan's nonadmirers would later describe him thus: "Like Fidel Castro, though on a lesser scale, Morgan was a superannuated juvenile delinquent ...")

After leaving prison, Morgan may have worked as a merchant seaman and in some aspect of electronics.

There had been plots and open insurrections against Batista in Cuba for a number of years; civil war was fully launched in November, 1956, with a major uprising in the eastern city of Santiago. One of the groups that organized to fight Batista was the *Directorio Revolucionario*, the militant arm of the Federation of University Students. It was with this group that Morgan made contact, possibly in Miami. He would later explain that he was impelled to involve himself because a friend had been tortured and killed by Batista's police. Quite likely Morgan was looking for new adventures; he was joining the rebels for the same reason so many Americans and foreigners have joined the French Foreign Legion.

Most foreigners became involved with Castro's 26 July Movement in Cuba, but Morgan made contact with the *Directorio Revolucionario* forces, led by El'oy Gutierrez Menoyo, in the Escambray mountains bisecting central Cuba.

The American adventurer impressed no one on his inauspicious arrival in the DR camp. As Roger Redondo, one of the original members of the group, recalls, "I was on my back with food for the troops when I heard people [at my camp] talking in English. It sounded to me like words I knew were bad words, like "son-of-a-bitch." I didn't speak English at that time. I snuck around trying to find out what the hell was going on in the camp.

"Lázaro Artola was with a great big American, all red, fat ... he had no shirt on. His body was stung by this 'chinicicacea.' It's a weed up there that has like a bee sting to it. His body was all puffed up, his eyes were puffed and he had scratches everywhere on him. Artola, who lived in that region for a long time, was immune to the weed, but Morgan was not.

"Artola said the American was an adventurer. He said, 'I brought him up to see how long he'll last. Because he's so fat, I don't think he'll last too long. He probably works for the CIA or FBI.' "

Menoyo ran the little band of guerrillas up and down the mountains for three days to get in shape. Morgan trudged up and down the mountains with the little twenty-nine-man band, losing weight and building up his strength. He lost thirty-five pounds quickly, since the fast-moving band was starving most of the time.

His military experience began to show. He had the training from the U.S. Army, and he taught the troops discipline. Ten days after they moved into the mountains, the small band encountered and ambushed a five-man Cuban army patrol. The patrol was preceding a major army sweep designed to clear out all revolutionary activity in the Escambray mountains. Flushed with their brief success, believed to be Morgan's first combat, the band force-marched over two hundred miles back and forth through the mountains for thirteen days, constantly exchanging shots with the larger pursuing force.

Morgan spoke no Spanish, so he had to communicate through Artola. As Redondo recalls: "Morgan would ask, 'How do you say this in Spanish?' pointing to everything he could find.

"That's how he started building his vocabulary, learning what the different things were. By the time the revolution was over, Morgan spoke pretty good Spanish."

By February 24, the guerrillas felt themselves safely enough ensconced to write a manifesto setting forth their military strategy—simultaneous urban and guerrilla warfare—and their political goals: restoration of democracy and a social revolution.

As revolutionary fervor grew throughout Cuba, the guerrilla group in the Escambray expanded too. Raw recruits as well as experienced urban fighters, all fleeing the police, marched up into the mountains to swell the ranks of the mountain warriors. There were encounters with the army at places with names like Fomento, Saltillo, Pedrero, Hanabanilla, and Güinía dé Miranda.

Morgan's interpretation of the Spanish language led to errors. "On one occasion, Eloy Menoyo ordered Morgan not to fire on an army patrol approaching our camp because he wanted prisoners," related Redondo. "Morgan did not understand, and as soon as the army patrol got within breathing range, he let loose. The patrol retreated and a couple of their men were killed, but Menoyo got upset because he wanted to take prisoners. As a result of this, the soldiers that did escape went out and got a very large force and they forced them to go through the mountains for many days."

Morgan told author Robert K. Brown the story of a near-fatal misunderstanding of the language: "I remember Eloy telling me something about "dos caminos" [two roads]. So I had my group of ten men move down one of the two roads stretching before us. A short while later, we were trapped in an army ambush. We fought some one hundred fifty soldiers for two and a half hours. We killed forty of them."

Morgan went on to say that he later found out Menoyo was ordering him not to proceed down the two roads. But that particular action was a turning point in Morgan's career. Everyone was impressed with the fact that he and his disciplined men had turned an ambush around and inflicted more casualties on the enemy force than they had inflicted on Morgan's band.

Morgan trained more and more revolutionaries in light infantry weapons and tactics, unarmed combat, and knife fighting, while leading forces in combat.

Redondo traced Morgan's Cuban military career: "He was commander of a guerrilla, which could be anywhere from five to twelve men. Later on, he was made commander of a column, and … later on he was made commander of a zone. He had become so useful … when he was trimmed down, with his military knowledge … he was speaking Spanish, that he was regarded as one of the most important members of the Second Front. In other words, every time there was anything important to be done where all the chiefs would meet, Morgan would be one of them."

Within a short time, troops led by Morgan had fought over fifteen major engagements, losing none of them.

As Morgan later related in an interview with author Brown: "The Cuban Army periodically sent out two thousand to three thousand troops in offensive thrusts into the mountains to hunt us down and destroy our small bands. We were always outnumbered at least thirty to one. Some twenty or thirty of us would stay on the soldiers' backs; we wouldn't let them alone. As soon as one group would break off another would take up the attack. That was how we had to fight. Why? We needed the guns."

Weapons were indeed a problem. The 26 July Movement was getting most of the foreign support going to the Cuban revolutionaries. Their public-relations personnel and contacts in the United States were better than any other group at the time. Even when weapons were shipped to the Second Front, Castro's men frequently managed to intercept them.

Morgan found an experienced gunsmith who had seen action in the Spanish Civil War and in a number of South American revolutions and intrigues. Captain Camacho, as he was called, scrounged up welding equipment, lathes, and a forge, to set up the revolution's army. He invented unique, effective weapons to compensate for the guerrillas' shortfall, making them out of parts available or captured locally. An inventive genius, one of his more widely known items was called the "Cuban-Winchester" (see picture on p. 10) by those who used it. He used the frame of a .44 lever action Winchester rifle produced in the 1890s and combined it with parts from Winchester semiautomatic rifles, M–1 Garand rifles, and a few handmade parts. He reamed out his own barrels and, depending on what ammo was available locally, the user could select .45 ACP, U.S. .30 carbine, or 9mm caliber by switching barrels. The weapon could utilize many different types of pistol magazines, including the efficient Luger .32 round "snail drum."

Morgan reported that this gun had limited accuracy, but was highly regarded due to its firepower. He himself preferred British 9mm submachine guns, due to their light weight and the light weight of the 9mm ammo. During his guerrilla experiences, he noted the difference a heavier gun and ammo made when trying to move fast and far.

The guerrillas were good at psychological warfare. On one occasion battle commands were broadcast over a shortwave radio in what Morgan later described as a "tremendous propaganda ploy." The rebel commander, Eloy Menoyo, "directed fictitious troops here and there, and had a helluva time." Realistic background noises were supplied by Morgan and others firing pistols, rifles, and Browning automatics. "We yelled a lot, too," said Morgan.

War in the Escambray mountains was brutal and vicious. When informers were found by Morgan's men, they would be executed on the spot and a sign left with one word: "Morgan." While revolutionaries in Cuba concentrated on dealing with Batista's army and secret police, the army and police terrorized the populace, further inflaming the people, who joined the rebels by the hundreds. As the flames of revolution spread, the army became more frustrated and repressive in its efforts to deal with the popular uprising.

Morgan related his experience of watching in hiding near a village with a seventeen-man group while an eighty-seven man Batista patrol systematically pillaged the village: the army men were drinking as they worked, and their depredations on the villagers became harder and harder for the outnumbered watchers to witness. Batista's men beat and tortured villagers for information on Morgan's band, who were only a few hundred feet away. The army men's anger increased as the villagers refused to talk, having no information to give them. From one of the last huts, a large, burly black sergeant pulled out a doddering, smiling, seventy-year-old man who was the village idiot. Unaware of the army men's anger, or of anything that was happening around him, the retarded old man smiled helpfully and suggested, "Why don't you go look for them in the mountains?" It was the wrong reply. Enraged, the big sergeant had his men hold the helpless, uncomprehending old man while he cut the man's lips off. Then they looped a noose around the mutilated and screaming old man's neck, tying the other end to a truck bumper. Laughing, the soldiers jumped in the vehicle and sped down the street with their helpless victim dragged behind.

The army patrol was followed, as its members moved drunkenly out of town. At an opportune moment the patrol was trapped by guerrillas and virtually annihilated, with only sixteen out of eighty-seven men making their way out alive. The large sergeant was captured alive. According to one witness, most of the guerrillas in that particular fight were carrying shotguns. "Everybody took a turn, and his [the sergeant's] body was just riddled with holes."

As Morgan later recalled, for up to eight miles there was nothing but blood, guts, and buzzards left following this long encounter with Batista's killers.

By the beginning of the summer the DR had captured the Escambray. So complete was the control that the rebels set up an administrative system. This included judicial, educational, and public works departments. By September there were some eight hundred guerrillas in the Escambray plus about one hundred fifty recruits in training. The guerrillas were supported by an extensive clandestine network in the urban areas. In the fall of 1958, the army made an attempt to cut the guerrilla-held area in two. The effort failed, and after two weeks the troops pulled out, leaving behind weapons, ammunition, and even a tank.

The DR now had two hospitals, two landing strips, and twenty-eight schools operating, as well as training camps all through the mountains. Morgan's fame

William Morgan at the Capri Hotel, Havana, Cuba, early 1959, holding one of his customized "Cuban-Winchesters"—a Winchester 94 converted to full automatic. (Photo by Robert K. Brown.)

rose as the DR attacked a fairly large city, Trinidad, with only four hundred rebels. Failing to take the city, the rebels fell back, with Morgan taking charge of the rear guard. His rear guard was successful in delaying a Batista army pursuing force, so the retreat was done in good order, preserving the morale of the rebels. Survivors of those early days remember how Morgan carried a wounded young rebel on his back all the way from the scene of the battle to the mountains, where he was treated.

All was not well, however, within the leadership of the DR. A division surfaced concerning tactics (whether to try to kill Batista; a DR attack on the Presidential Palace in March, 1957 had failed) and over who was in command of the guerrilla fighters.

Menoyo broke away from the DR and set up a separate guerrilla organization, called the *Segundo Frente Nacional del Escambray* (the Second National Front of the Escambray). With Menoyo went Morgan, serving as a close aide. Both men were now *Comandantes* (major/commander), highest rank among any of the guerrillas fighting Batista, and there were approximately 300 men under Menoyo's command. The Second Front soon distinguished itself in the war. In an encounter at La Diana it inflicted 37 casualties on the army; at Charco Azul, the army suffered 140 military casualties. There were additional clashes, each enabling the Second Front further to consolidate and extend its control, and to become better known.

Friction grew between the Second Front and the more publicized 26 July Movement led by Fidel Castro. Eloy Gutierrez Menoyo was a true revolutionary, dedicated to the idea of social change and democracy. His brother had fought in the Spanish Civil War and in Africa, with the French Foreign Legion, while another had been killed during the attack on Batista's Presidential Palace in 1957. Menoyo knew a little about Castro—enough to know that Castro might be as repressive as Batista. In fact, Menoyo considered Castro a potential dictator. Morgan was anticommunist and cautious of anyone who had leftist leanings. He was remembered by his compatriots for the American flag patch he wore on his uniform at all times.

Hence, both men were concerned at the direction in which the 26 July Movement was going. The 26 July Movement was concerned about the strategically well-placed Second Front as well.

Castro dispatched Ernesto "Che" Guevara with a column of two hundred men, ostensibly to join Morgan's forces in Escambray and to coordinate First and Second Front action. In fact, according to intelligence received by Menoyo and Morgan, the force was tasked to take control of the Second Front.

Che's column was sent on ahead to effect a linkup with Morgan and Menoyo's men while Che dealt with other business. But Morgan and his men surrounded Che's two hundred men and disarmed them. When Che arrived, hot words were exchanged as negotiations began. He was humiliated by the disarming of his men by the Morgan-trained guerrillas and further humiliated when rules were laid down that effectively precluded his men from crossing into what became Second Front–dominated territory. The final straw came when the Escambray guerrillas returned Che's men to him weaponless and without boots.

Morgan, Menoyo, and Castro tried to work out an arrangement to avoid civil war between the groups before the goal of overthrowing Batista was met. They ended up with a plan to coordinate military actions and social plans for the people under their control. The two groups were to coordinate activities in the future.

By this time, Morgan had a $20,000 price tag on his head—dead or alive—from the Batista government. But the government was tottering. On December 22, 1958, Morgan planned and led a large rebel attack on a key fortified area protecting Cienfuegos, one of Cuba's largest cities. The rebels surrounded the fortress—a converted tuberculosis sanitarium called Topes de Collantes—and cut it off from all outside communication and supply. Unable to attack owing to their lack of artillery, the rebels simply kept the pressure on, letting nature take its course inside the fortress. In six days, the fortress was surrendered and the road was open to Cienfuegos.

The victory signaled the beginning of the end for Batista's army. A three thousand-man column was formed, with Morgan planning to attack and take Cienfuegos on January 2, 1959; but word came on January 1 that Batista and some

Comandante Morgan, the highest-ranking American to serve with the anti-Batista forces in Cuba, is shown (far right) in the Sierra Escambray mountains with (left to right) Nene Français (killed in the battle of Trinidad); Comandante Eloy Gutierrez Menoyo (jailed in Cuba); Jose Garcia, kneeling (killed in Cuba); and Henry Fuerte (killed in Haitian invasion, 1959). (Private collection of Roger Redondo.)

of his entourage had fled the country in the early morning hours, leaving Batista's army and supporters to fend for themselves.

Batista left just after midnight on New Year's Day. Morgan and his column took the city and major naval base at Cienfuegos at 8:00 A.M. the same morning, and Morgan became the "mayor" of the city.

When Castro arrived in Cienfuegos on his victory trip west to Havana, he was greeted by Morgan. Author Jay Mallin recalls: "Morgan was a good host. He let Castro do all the talking and hog the spotlight."

Although at first he held only the vague title "Delegate General of the President to the Armed Organizations," Castro quickly emerged as the dominant figure in the new government and in the country—a position he would still hold twenty years later. Castro was, in effect, commander-in-chief of the country's military and, as such, he wanted no armed men on the island except those that he commanded. The Second Front of the Escambray and other revolutionary organizations were dissolved, the rebels being given the option of becoming part of the regular—now "revolutionary"—armed forces. Morgan stayed, maintaining his rank of *comandante* and his salary of 277 pesos monthly.

For a while, Morgan and his followers celebrated their victory. Offers for movies and books came in, but nothing was done about them. Then Morgan decided to return to Las Villas Province, his base area during the revolution. He threw himself into rebuilding projects, trying to repair the damage caused by years of neglect and war. He and Menoyo formed a veterans' organization, designed to monitor the progress of the revolution and prevent it from drifting away from democracy into another tyranny.

It was a time of violent ferment in Cuba. The entire civilian and military leadership of the country had changed. The political structure had been radically altered, and major social transformations were underway. Although this was not apparent initially, the country was on the road to communism. Exiles from other countries flooded into Cuba. Flushed with victory, Castro and his men aimed at spreading their revolution to other countries, utilizing these exiles. The exiles received military training, were armed, and then were dispatched to invade their homelands. One of the major invasions, by land and air, was that of the Dominican Republic, in an effort to topple the dictator Generalissimo Rafael Leonidas Trujillo. The invasion was crushed. Trujillo never forgave Castro.

It was a time of intrigue, and some of the intrigue was directed against Castro, too. Not every Cuban, by far, was euphoric over his coming to power. A conspiracy began to take form, involving dissident civilians, former military men, and military men who had served under the Batista regime but, not having war crimes charged against them, had been permitted to remain in service.

The plotters contacted Morgan and Menoyo and asked them to join the conspiracy. The pitch was probably that Cuba was. heading left and away from the democratic

Rebels gathered at Menoyo's home in Havana, early 1959. Morgan is second from right, standing; to his left, Menoyo's mother; to her left, Menoyo. (Private collection of Roger Redondo.)

ideals for which the revolution had been fought. Morgan, Menoyo, and their men had battled for democracy; would they not fight again now? One of the plot leaders was Arturo Hernandez Tellaheche, a former Cuban senator. He was to become president of the country if the plot succeeded.

Morgan and Menoyo agreed to go along with the conspiracy. At some point, however, they contacted Castro and informed him of their role. Whether they did this out of loyalty or in self-preservation because Castro had learned about the plot is not known. It is also possible that Morgan and Menoyo turned double agents because the United States failed to support the plot after Morgan made an approach to the U.S. embassy. Morgan told an Embassy official, Paul Bethel: "Castro is a Communist, see, and we don't like Communists....Well, we've been working to get our people into strategic spots. One of them is secretary to Che [Guevara]." Morgan claimed that his forces, with adequate arms and ammunition, could overthrow Castro "within three days."

The United States stayed clear, perhaps fearing that this was a trap. Perhaps the Americans missed a good chance to be rid of Castro; no one will ever know.

Some observers or colleagues felt that Morgan was in the plot from its inception, and turned traitor when Castro got wind of it, fearing for his own life. Others wondered if the whole plot wasn't instigated by Castro to flush out his opposition once and for all, and that Morgan helped get it going for Castro. Castro's later treatment of Morgan would indicate trust and gratitude at first, coupled with growing doubts as reports of Morgan's alleged counter-revolutionary activities trickled in later.

Lurking off to one side in the conspiratorial shadows was the Dominican Republic's Trujillo. Cuban exiles living in the DomRep were in contact with the plotters. Trujillo's own hand in the affair was so direct that Morgan was advised to go to Miami to pick up funds from the Dominican consul there. He did so, receiving $52,000 from the consul to assist the conspiracy. Trujillo sent a shipload of weapons to Cuba which included at least twenty .50 caliber machine guns. The plot called for anti-Castro troops to seize Havana, to be followed by the landing of an expeditionary force from the DomRep.

The time to strike approached; little did the plotters know that Castro was aware of every step they took. On a Saturday in August, 1959, the leaders of the conspiracy gathered in Morgan's house in the Miramar suburb of Havana. Castro, pretending to be unaware of the plot, flew that same day to the Isle of Pines, where he frequently vacationed. (The plotters had expected Castro to be out of the country altogether, participating in an international conference in Chile. He didn't go there—that would have been a bit *too* dangerous.)

And then the blow fell, Morgan and Menoyo, instead of continuing in the conspiracy, announced that everyone was under arrest. Before the stunned eyes of the conspirators, Castro himself and a top military commander strode in. The commander sarcastically said to plot leader Tellaheche, "Any orders, Mr. President?"

Castro went around asking each of the plotters, "What were you going to be minister of?" The plotters were taken to military headquarters, and a nationwide roundup of other suspects was launched.

Morgan and Menoyo had performed a major service for Castro. Not only had they helped destroy a substantial plot, they had enabled Castro to clear out the last holdovers in the army, leaving only his own men there. Castro was now deeply entrenched in control, a fact which would enable him to weather the Bay of Pigs invasion a year and eight months later.

A strange thing now happened. Trujillo was a canny leader who had succeeded in running his country for almost three decades, despite international disfavor. But now he displayed an unexpected lack of intuition and/or intelligence—intelligence of both the mental and the military kinds.

The Cuban government said nothing about the conspiracy. Rumors swirled throughout the country, however, and it was known that an extensive purge was underway. Then, on August 11, 1959, the *Miami News* carried a story by Mallin providing a detailed account of the conspiracy and of the arrest of the leaders. The story was picked up and relayed by Associated Press and carried by the major Havana dailies. That the plot leaders had been seized must certainly have been known in Ciudad Trujillo, capital of the Dominican Republic.

But despite this, Trujillo went ahead with the plans for an invasion of Cuba. Morgan did his best to encourage him....

Following the arrest of the conspirators, Morgan and Menoyo flew to Las Villas Province, site of their original guerrilla operations. Cuban newspapers carried veiled speculation about Morgan. Was he a hero or a traitor? The uncertainty enhanced a new, crucial role upon which Morgan was about to embark.

Using the code name "Henry," Morgan began broadcasting by shortwave radio to the Dominican Republic. He reported that troops of the Second Front of the Escambray were in control of southern Las Villas, except for the cities. "Our troops are advancing," said Henry. "Send the [Dominican] Legion."

"Forward, Henry!" urged the Dominicans. And the Dominican radio claimed, "Contrary to the allegations of Fidel, Morgan is in Las Villas at the head of the counter-revolution."

An additional indication came that Trujillo was swallowing the bait. A plane circled over an isolated stretch of the Las Villas coast known as Playa El Inglés. It parachuted down cases of .50 caliber ammunition.

Castro went to great lengths to convince Trujillo that Morgan was telling the truth and that an uprising was indeed underway. All telephone communications with Las Villas were cut. "The line is interrupted," phone operators told persons trying to make calls. The Cuban army blocked the highway between Cienfuegos and the town of Trinidad—where the "rebels" were supposedly in control—and let no civilian traffic through to the latter town.

Castro flew to the airport at Cienfuegos in his transport plane and immediately took off in an army helicopter. Newspapermen who tried to find out what was happening received blank looks from army officers. It was obvious that Castro couldn't fly far in a helicopter, so the newsmen reported that "he was flying over the hills of Trinidad." The implication was that he couldn't land at Trinidad itself. The press began carrying reports that Castro was personally directing the fight against the counter-revolutionaries.

All of this convinced Trujillo's otherwise astute intelligence service. The Dominicans informed "Henry" by radio that a plane would be sent to Trinidad carrying weapons and emissaries. In the evening of August 12, lights were lit along the small airstrip outside Trinidad. Morgan and Menoyo waited in a shack. Troops ringed the field. Castro sat in the dark under a mango tree.

Sure enough, shortly after eight o'clock a C–46 winged in and came to a stop. Out stepped six men. One wore the habit of a priest. The others wore mufti or khaki pants and white shirts. Morgan and Menoyo greeted the men sent by Trujillo and led them to a *cuartel* about half a mile up the road to confer. The carefully coached Cuban troops set up cries of "Death to Castro!" and "Viva Trujillo!" The troops unloaded the plane, which had brought thirteen bazookas, twenty cases of bazooka shells, and twenty cases of .50 caliber ammunition, as well as gloves to be used in firing bazookas. Castro himself slipped off his jacket and wanted to help unload but was deterred by prudent aides.

Once the cargo was off and the conference completed, the emissaries reboarded, and the aircraft took off again. Morgan and Menoyo were told that the plane would be back the following night with men and more weapons.

It was carnival time in Cienfuegos. People danced in the streets and houses were festooned with palm fronds and pieces of brightly colored paper. After the C–46 had left, Castro slipped into town and went to the home of a city commissioner. The next day a puzzled Cienfueguero noticed a soldier pacing up and down a portion of a sidewalk. The worried citizen called military headquarters and reported, "There is a crazy soldier here doing strange things." Actually, it was a sentry doing duty outside the house where Castro was staying. The word soon spread that Castro was in town, and a crowd gathered in front of the house. Castro stepped onto a balcony and was loudly cheered. This was his thirty-third birthday, and the crowd broke into *Happy Birthday*. Castro told the citizens: "Go to the carnival and dance and enjoy yourselves. Tonight I will be with you."

There was unusual activity at the Cienfuegos airport. Five transport planes flew in carrying approximately sixty-five troops each. The soldiers boarded trucks and set out for Trinidad. Castro disappeared from the house in which he had been staying.

The troop trucks rolled through the green hills around Cienfuegos and into Trinidad. Trinidad, with cobblestoned streets and shingled houses set next to each other, has hardly changed since Spanish colonial days. It was here that the final act of the great intrigue was about to played out.

Curious citizens stood on the sidewalks and watched the troops rolling by and waved to them. The troops were stationed around the airport and on the road between the field and the *cuartel*. Townspeople gathered along the side of the road. The scene of the previous night was repeated. The airport lights were lit. Morgan and Menoyo waited in the shack. Castro stood off to one side about fifty yards from the airstrip.

At about 8:30 p.m. the C–46 appeared again. It landed and came to a stop a few yards away from the shack. Grim men wearing olive green uniforms stepped from the plane, and the waiting troops again yelled, "Down with Fidel!" *"Vive el jefe!,"* "Down with the revolution!" Castro happily joined in (later he would comment, "But I couldn't bring myself to say *"Viva Trujillo!"*).

Morgan and Menoyo greeted the expeditionaries and again led them to the shack. Now, however. the drama drew to a close. The expeditionaries suddenly found themselves facing drawn guns and, dumbfounded, were told they were under arrest.

Still remaining at the plane, however, were two expeditionaries and the pilot, Colonel Jose Antonio Soto, who had been Batista's personal pilot and assistant chief of the Cuban air force. The unloading of the plane proceeded. The troops removed cases of ammunition and hand grenades, Springfield rifles, and Thompson submachine guns (their serial numbers carefully filed off). One of the expeditionaries handed a soldier a Dominican dollar as a souvenir. Another gave a lieutenant a major's stars and jokingly "promoted" him.

Once the plane had been unloaded, Cuban soldiers entered it to arrest the remaining expeditionaries. Someone started shooting, and within seconds the aircraft and the surrounding area were filled with confused gunfire. Castro stood nearby directing his men. When the firing ended, two expeditionaries and two soldiers were dead and several soldiers were wounded. Among the eight captured expeditionaries were several prizes: the son of a former mayor of Havana, the son of a former high police official, and Alfredo Maliban, a Spaniard who had once served in the French Foreign Legion and was now a member of Trujillo's Dominican Legion.

A few nights later Castro, as was his wont, appeared on television and paraded his prisoners. Castro boasted, "If we could have kept our plans secret for fifteen days we would have captured Trujillo and his whole army!"

Castro used the incident to lock up all his opponents, whether they advanced revolution against him or were simply vocal non-believers in the new Marxist faith. The arrests continued until up to six thousand suspected anti-Castro opponents were picked up.

Trujillo's memory was long, and assassins were sent after Morgan, but they failed to accomplish their task.

The Second Front on parade one year after the revolution. Left to right: Comandante Armando Fleites, Captain Roger Redondo (in bush hat), Comandante Menoyo, man with flag unidentified. (Private collection of Roger Redondo.)

William Morgan had closed another chapter in his life. There were now no new adventures in sight. He remained a *comandante* but he commanded no troops. Was there, perhaps, a lingering suspicion in Castro's mind? Morgan himself would later say, "Some of the other *comandantes* were jealous. They resented the fact that an American held the rank of *comandante*. They resented the publicity that I got. If I had wanted to command a regiment in Las Villas I would have gotten it. But Fidel would have stayed up all night worrying about me. A guy in the middle can so easily get caught."

Morgan ostensibly decided to get out of politics and out of suspicion's way. He took a job with the Agriculture Ministry managing a huge fish hatchery (carp, sunfish, black bass) outside Havana. And then the soldier of fortune became interested in an even more unlikely subject: the raising of frogs. He read up on the subject and talked the agriculture minister into investing $70,000 in frogs, labor, and materials. It was figured that the exportation of frogs would bring Cuba foreign exchange. The site selected for the frog farm was a large *finca* southwest of Havana that had been expropriated from the former top labor leader under the Batista government. Morgan planned out the farm itself and supervised the digging of ditches and building of concrete tanks. The farm was started in March, 1960 and, two months later, Morgan had half a million scampering, croaking frogs. The man who had commanded troops in battle now managed one hundred workers, all of whom addressed him simply as "William."

Morgan took his work seriously. He decided the type and quantity of plants to be purchased to provide shade for the frogs in the ditches. He decided the chemicals to be used in the tanks in which the skins were placed. He kept the books, approved any purchases to be made, and arranged with canners as to the quantities of legs they were to receive and the prices they were to pay. Asked whether he had used blueprints in planning the ditches, Morgan replied: "Blueprints, your ass. I dug those fucking ditches."

While setting up and running his frog farm, Morgan continued managing the fish hatchery some twenty miles away. The two places were linked by shortwave radio. Morgan was kept busy: "I work eighteen hours daily, including Sundays. When I get to my horne in Havana at night I drop into bed."

Morgan knew that Trujillo was "a guy that never forgives." Morgan claimed that the Dominican generalissimo was "offering five hundred thousand dollars for me dead." At his hip Morgan wore a gold-plated .45 with a bullet ready in the chamber. Wherever he went he was followed by Tommygun-toting bodyguards, "my boys." Said Morgan: "We shoot fifty to sixty rounds in practice every week. Someone said to me that he wouldn't like to issue insurance on me. I said I wouldn't like to be the guy who tries to collect."

Comandantes Menoyo and Morgan leaving Havana after meeting with Castro, spring of 1959. Stars on their epaulets signify their rank, highest in the Cuban Revolutionary Army. (Private collection of Roger Redondo.)

This was mid-1960, and Cuba was now well on its way toward becoming a communist state. Morgan was unabashed about his own views: "There isn't anyone in Cuba who doesn't know where I stand—Fidel, Raul, or anyone. I am anticommunist. I don't like them. They tried to hold a political meeting here and I threw them out." What if the Cuban government were to change? he was asked. Morgan, whose U.S. citizenship had been lifted because he had served in a foreign army, responded: "I've run out of countries. I guess I'd have to go back into the hills."

Some mornings Morgan would line up his workers in military formation and shout: "I hate all communists! They work for Russia, not for Cuba. All of you who are communists and work for Russia take one step forward." Of course, no one did.

Morgan expressed the belief to Mallin, who visited him at the frog farm, that Castro would never let anything happen to him at the hands of the communists. It was a misplaced trust.

Rumors were ripe that Morgan was active again in an anti-Castro plot while running the frog farm. The rumors may have had some veracity, since close associates reported years later that his "frog farm" began to look more and more like a military camp. He hired his Second Front friends, and his farm trucks may have been used to transport arms and supplies concealed in fifty-five-gallon oil drums to anti-Castro guerrillas in the Escambray mountains. Strong guerrilla forces opposed to Castro's slide to tyranny were operating against Castro's army.

Max Lesnick, a Cuban journalist, recalled later, "We told Morgan he might be infiltrated by Castro's spies—and he was. He was operating against Castro in the same manner as against Batista. He was the mastermind of the uprising in the Escambray mountains before the Bay of Pigs, something he has never received credit for. All the Escambray rebels were in some way connected with him. Was the CIA involved? One cannot say for certain. If Morgan was involved with the CIA then we might assume the CIA was involved in the Escambray effort."

The chief of staff of the Cuban army was to be married, and Morgan took a woman's bag made of frog skins to the chief's office as a gift for the bride. As Morgan entered the office, he was seized and disarmed. He was then imprisoned. The following day an item in the official daily *Revolución* reported that "*Comandante* William Morgan has been using military trucks under his command illegally to transport food and ammunition into the Escambray Mountains." The paper said that Morgan had been arrested for counter-revolutionary activities.

Morgan was sent to the dreary, dreaded La Cabaña prison across the bay from Havana. He would rise at dawn, do calisthenics, then march around the compound shouting commands at himself. When it was time for his trial, he went to it singing, "As the caissons go rolling along." Morgan was found guilty and sentenced to death.

But the famed guerrilla leader was not without teeth. According to an account that later surfaced, Morgan was smuggled a Colt .45 pistol by a visitor. Morgan knew that Castro occasionally visited the prison. Cuban intelligence wanted information on the Escambray revolutionaries from Morgan. Morgan refused to speak to anyone but Fidel Castro about the subject. Castro visited the prison and approached Morgan's cell. The cell door was solid, with a small window. Castro said, "Morgan, what do you want to tell me?" and Morgan replied, "If you come here I will tell you all I know." Castro would not go inside Morgan's cell, and Morgan was unable to draw him into the line of fire. Apparently, Morgan thought to wait for another chance, and so he kept the pistol concealed. The pistol was allegedly found during a search of his cell after Morgan was shot.

There are two versions of the story of Morgan's death. In those days, prisoners to be executed were not told when they were going to be shot. They would be taken out of their cells to undergo further "routine interrogation" or "to go to the dentist," only to suddenly find themselves facing a firing squad.

According to one version, on March 11 Morgan was marched out of the cell at La Cabaña and stood against a dry moat. Fidel and Raul Castro were present. It was 2:30 A.M. Lights were beamed on Morgan.

As Morgan's hands were being tied behind his back, a voice shouted from behind the lights, "Kneel and beg for your life!" Morgan shouted back, "I kneel for no man!"

Not a firing squad but a single marksman was used. He sadistically put a bullet through one of Morgan's knees, then another through the other knee. Morgan fell to the ground cursing the communists. "There!" exulted the voice. "You see, we made you kneel!" The rifleman put a bullet through one of Morgan's shoulders, then took his time putting a bullet into the other. Finally, a merciful captain walked up to Morgan and ended his agony by emptying a magazine from his Tommygun into the American's chest.

The other version of Morgan's execution had Morgan embrace the commander of the firing squad immediately prior to his execution, to show he held no grudge against the man doing his job. The symbolic act, if it occurred, added to Morgan's stature as a brave commander to many of the ritual-conscious Cubans.

In this version, as told to the authors by a foreign national who served fourteen years in Castro's prisons after fighting for the revolution, Morgan then embraced each member of the firing squad, letting them know he held no grudges against them for doing what they were ordered. Morgan refused a blindfold and refused to die on his knees, as ordered. Two men in the firing squad were ordered to shoot Morgan in the legs to force him to his knees, but the bullets failed to strike bone. The rest of the firing squad finished him off standing up.

Whichever version is true, it is apparent that Morgan won additional respect from his friends and opponents alike in the brave way he faced death.

Three years earlier, shortly after coming to Cuba, Morgan had sent *New York Times* reporter Herbert Matthews a "credo" titled "Why am I here." Morgan had written, "I cannot say I have always been a good citizen, but being here I can appreciate the way of life that is ours from birth. And here I can realize the dedication to justice and liberty it takes for men to live and fight as these men do whose only possible pay or reward is a free country....

"Over the years we as Americans have found that dictators and communist [*sic*] are bad people with whom to do business yet here is a dictator who has been supported by the communist and he would fall from power tomorrow if it were not for the American aid. And I ask myself why do we support those who would destroy in other lands the ideals which we hold so dear?"

William Morgan fought and died in a foreign land, but he was never anything other than an American.

CHAPTER 3

David "Mickey" Marcus: A True Hero

Everything he did, he did superbly. Amateur prize fighter, West Point graduate, prison official, military planner, warrior—he was always tops. And when it came time to help defend a brand-new nation, Mickey Marcus did that splendidly, too. In recent centuries probably only the Marquis de Lafayette has played a comparable role as a soldier of fortune.

But if they would eventually play significantly parallel military roles, the beginnings of the Marquis and of Marcus were notably different. The Marquis was born into a wealthy, aristocratic French family; before he was twenty, he held a captaincy of dragoons at the French court. He added to the family fortune by marrying a wealthy woman, thus becoming one of the richest men in France.

David Daniel "Mickey" Marcus was born on Washington's birthday, 1902, the fifth child of an immigrant Jewish couple from Rumania. The family lived in New York's poverty-stricken Lower East Side, and the father, Mordecai, made his living selling vegetables from a pushcart. Mordecai did well, however, and the family was able to move to a better neighborhood in Brooklyn.

Mickey had just turned eight when misfortune befell the family: Mordecai died of illness. Again the family had to move, this time to a less agreeable Brooklyn neighborhood, the Brownsville district. This was a section where hoodlums delighted in tormenting Jews, particularly elders on the elevated train. Mickey's older brother "Big Mike" organized a group of husky Jewish youngsters and led raids against the hoodlums. It was a lesson that Mickey would never forget.

Mickey was repeatedly to learn that Jews had to fight back against tormentors and not be complacent victims. Sent for two weeks to a summer camp for underprivileged children, he was subject to frequent attacks by anti-Semitic youngsters. He always fought back, even when being knocked flat would be the inevitable result. Later he told a friend: "I'm going to build up my body. I'm going to make myself so tough that I can handle myself against anybody, anywhere."

Mickey's brother "Big Mike" was a gym fan, and so young Mickey took to accompanying him in his gymnastics. He learned to use his fists and was thoroughly at home on the rings and parallel bars. Following his brother around, young Marcus became known as "Little Mike." This later became "Mickey," the name by which he would ever after be best known.

Mickey attended Public School 109, and at the urgings of his religious mother, he also studied the Torah at his temple's school. The Torah is the fundamental Jewish legal code, developed from the five Books of Moses by early rabbis and with learned commentaries appended by later sages. It is a highly moral document, setting forth wisdom for living a good life. This was Mickey's first absorption of law, and it would be law that formed the framework within which his own life developed.

Mickey was a good student, the scholar of the family. He entered Boys' High, where he was elected to the honorary scholastic society, Arista. He was still quick to get into a fight over a point of honor, but he also burned off energy as a top athlete. The workouts in the gym paid off: he won letters in track and baseball and was a crack first baseman on the school baseball team.

And just as Lafayette had while still in his teens decided upon a military career, so did Mickey Marcus, and the route he chose was the U.S. Military Academy at West Point. A number of factors evidently influenced Mickey's decision: He was impressed by films of the cadets he saw in the movies; a close friend was going to West Point; military life appealed to the scrappy and athletic young man; and being a West Pointer would mean that the first-generation American had truly become a part of the America he loved. In June, 1920, Mickey Marcus entered West Point and launched his career. (The Academy superintendent at the time: Brigadier General Douglas MacArthur.)

West Point Cadet David Marcus (about 1924). (Courtesy of U.S. Military Archives.)

The harassments visited upon helpless first-year plebes at West Point are well known. But for the young man who had been early able to handle anti-Semitic viciousness, these difficulties offered no great problem. He achieved the reputation of being the most insouciant of plebes. A friend wrote in a letter, "[Mickey] just laughs at every upperclassman who tries to crawl [harass] him." Upperclassmen would sternly discipline Mickey, he would do as told—and then his grin would become a laugh, and the upperclassman would, despite his best efforts, find himself laughing, too.

Mickey fit perfectly into West Point. The ethics of the Point corresponded with the teachings of the Torah. The adventure of military life gave a purpose to Mickey's rambunctiousness. But Mickey was also a scholar, and the Point gave him the opportunity to study. Upon graduation in 1924, he was in the top third of his class, particularly strong in the study of class campaigns and at the same time displaying what the Academy called "Leadership Potential." As an athlete, Mickey exercised his prowess in gymnastics and in the boxing ring at the Point. (And still the spirit and skill exceeded the body. For one important fight, Mickey was barely able to meet the 135-pound requirement in the lightweight division.)

Mickey had met a young lady named Emma while at the Point, and he courted her. They were married on July 3, 1927, Mickey proudly wearing his uniform. After graduation from the. Point, Mickey served on Governor's Island in New York Bay. In addition to his military duties, he returned to the study of law and spent three years attending classes at a night law school. His next post was to be in Puerto Rico, but Mickey and Emma decided they did not want to live there, preferring that Mickey begin a career in law. So he resigned his army commission and worked as a law clerk, waiting until his admission to the bar.

Mickey moved into parallel legal and political careers. He entered governmental service, working for the Treasury Department and then in the U.S. Attorney's office, where he came to know a lawyer named Thomas E. Dewey. Mickey was a prosecutor in Prohibition cases. He also involved himself in local Republican affairs and in civic projects. Emma worked as a teacher.

A reform administration headed by the fiery congressman, Fiorello La Guardia, came into power in New York, and Mickey was named first deputy commissioner of correction. Under years of Tammany Hall rule, the prisons of New York City had become cesspools of corruption. Mickey set about cleaning up the problem with a "large broom." One of the worst spots was the penitentiary on Welfare Island, which had virtually been taken over by gangsters and was being run like a convict country club. Mickey studied the situation, drew up a battle plan, and put together a seventy-one-man force. He then personally led a raid on the prison which smashed the underworld hold on it—and won national attention for Mickey and the reform administration. Although he was technically deputy commissioner, Mickey actually ran the correction department, because of the illness of the commissioner and the friendship that had developed between Mickey and La Guardia, himself a man of

Lieutenant Marcus and his bride Emma, July 3, 1927. (Private collection.)

action. Eventually Mickey would become commissioner, thus officially achieving the position he actually held anyway.

Mickey cleaned up the prisons, but his vision went far beyond that. He brought in the first full-time psychiatrist. He advocated creation of a "separate colony" where drug addicts could be treated. For juvenile offenders he urged establishment of work and study communities in the countryside. Always there was the compassionate side of Mickey Marcus: for the suffering wife or sister of a convict, there was often financial assistance direct from Mickey's own pocket.

Mickey was clearly a rising figure in the affairs of what was then the world's largest city. But this was to be only an interlude of civilian service. War was raging in Europe, and it was a fair bet that the United States would sooner or later become involved. Mickey decided to return to the army. He had kept a Reserve commission when he left the regular army. This commission had been with the field artillery but later, in view of Mickey's legal background, it was shifted to the judge advocate general's department. Hitler was supreme in much of Europe already, but this was not a determining factor in Mickey's decision to rejoin active service. He stated strongly: "It's got nothing to do with my being a Jew. I've always thought of myself as an American—an American who happens to be of the Jewish faith. I'd feel the same way about Hitler if he was pushing Buddhists around, or Seventh-day Adventists. An attack on any religion is an attack on all of them." At West Point Mickey had

Magistrate Marcus: at thirty-four, the youngest judge on the New York bench, 1936. (Private collection.)

roomed with an Episcopalian and a Roman Catholic who became two of his closest friends. He came to refer to himself as an "Episcopal Jew."

Back in uniform, Mickey was sent to a training camp in Alabama in 1940, with the federally activated National Guard unit to which he was attached. He held the rank of lieutenant colonel and his post was that of judge advocate of the 27th Infantry Division. Although legal officers were not supposed to command troops in the field, Mickey was able to obtain authorization to lead a unit in the Louisiana maneuvers during the summer of 1941. He did such an outstanding job that he was recommended for promotion to full colonel; the recommendation stated that he was a "very virile executive, an allaround able and forceful commander."

Then came Pearl Harbor. Mickey turned down a Pentagon assignment in favor of going with his division to the Pacific. He wrote to Emma, "War will bring the midnight of civilization. Yet we must learn never to grieve over the dead body of some mother's son, but only over a defunct American democracy ... America, the only country on this earth whose existence rests on the heritage of ideas, not the magic of blood ancestry."

The task of the 27th Division was to defend war-battered and endangered Hawaii. Mickey served as executive officer but later was assigned to set up and command a Rangers' Training School, where two hundred men at a time would go through eight-week courses designed to prepare them for the jungle warfare that was part of the vast conflict in the Pacific. Mickey trained some eight thousand men—men who in their months of combat earned a special reputation for toughnēss and fighting ability.

Mickey hoped for a command post with his Rangers. Instead he found himself brought back to the USA in 1943 to serve with the Pentagon's Civil Affairs Division. With the new job came a full colonelcy. The CAD was concerned with the governing of lands captured by the advancing Allied forces. One of Mickey's more gratifying tasks: to draw up the terms for Italy's surrender. Later, even more satisfying, he drew up a draft for Nazi Germany's unconditional surrender. The Jewish boy from the Lower East Side had come a far way indeed.

In fact, Mickey Marcus walked with the greats. His duties took him to the Roosevelt-Churchill-Chiang meeting in Cairo in November, 1943. Then he went on to Teheran for the Roosevelt and Churchill meeting with Stalin (of whom Mickey noted, "He made his own decisions and he made them fast—without bothering to be tactful"); then to the conference at Dumbarton Oaks, where the foundations for the United Nations were laid. When, later, Roosevelt and Churchill conferred at Quebec, Mickey Marcus was there again. From this meeting Mickey kept as a memento a list

Colonel Marcus (right) receives the Distinguished Service Medal from Major General John H. Hilldring in Washington, 1945. (Courtesy of U.S. Army.)

limiting to six American officers the distribution of ultrasecret documents. On the list were the chiefs of staff of the Army, Navy, Army Air Force, Roosevelt's personal chief of staff, a lieutenant general who was a top staff officer—and Colonel Marcus. And then at Yalta, another historic Allied meeting, Mickey was again present and participating. Immediately after the war, he attended the Potsdam conference, too.

Despite the importance of his staff work, Mickey was not about to go through World War II without being in the frontlines at least once. The year was 1944 and the Allies were preparing to crack Hitler's Fortress Europe, and in Washington Mickey chafed at his desk job. Finally he wangled a trip to London, officially to improve communications between the Civil Affairs Division and Supreme Headquarters Allied Expeditionary Force (SHAEF). At SHAEF Mickey tackled the CAD's concerns regarding what the Allies expected would be the reoccupation of Europe.

On this trip, however, Mickey had his mind on other matters in addition to the administration of conquered territories. He knew that the U.S. 101st Airborne Division would be one of the paratroop divisions jumping into occupied Europe to initiate the Allied invasion. The day before D-Day, as the troops of the 101st were boarding their planes in southern England, Mickey came up waving official papers, and joined the men aboard a C–46. He was now part of the largest airborne attack force in history—two American and one British airborne divisions in hundreds of planes and gliders. The records indicate that Mickey was one of only two men present who had never parachuted before (the other was a staff officer).

At a little past midnight on June 6, 1944, Mickey made his combat jump into Nazi-occupied France. He landed in an open field. The paratroopers had been supplied with toy soundmakers that reproduced the sound of a cricket, so that the troops could identify themselves in the darkness. These were used to good avail, and Mickey rounded up enough men to make two patrols, one of which he commanded. When a German machine gun opened fire, Mickey and his men went into action. Moving about and firing with an automatic rifle, Mickey distracted the Germans until his patrol could sweep down on them. Six Germans were killed.

In the ensuing days, as the Allies battled to hold their ground and the Germans tried to dislodge them, Mickey was in the midst of the combat, very much an active participant. In one engagement he killed four enemy soldiers. On another occasion he prevented a group of paratroopers from falling into a German trap—he noticed that the "cricket" chirps enticing them forward were spaced oddly, as if the soundmakers were being used by persons not familiar with them. Instead of being captured, the paratroopers, led by Mickey, rounded up a band of German riflemen and freed several Yanks that the Germans were holding. Mickey's biographer, Ted Berkman, has noted: "As the campaign progressed, legends began to circulate about a brandy-swigging, gorilla-chested Civil Affairs colonel who bounced like a brawny Pan through the countryside, here joining a combat outfit for a few days, there lingering in a newly occupied village to help set up a military government."

The commander of the 101st Airborne, Major General Maxwell Taylor, was startled to come upon Mickey—they had been students together at West Point—at the frontlines. Asked Taylor, "What the hell are *you* doing here?" Replied Mickey casually, "Oh—just looking around." Taylor later remarked that he "couldn't help having a sneaking admiration for a guy who went this far out of his way to be where the war was, when he could have been parked in a comfortable hotel room in London."

Word of Mickey's activities reached his commander in Washington. Major General John Hilldring, and orders went back out to Mickey to return immediately to Washington. Without time to change his battle-worn uniform, Mickey was put aboard a plane to London and then another that flew him back to the States. The fighting part of the war was over for Mickey Marcus.

Mickey continued to work for Civil Affairs until a little less than a year later, when he was transferred to the military occupation staff in Germany. Before leaving Washington, Mickey was awarded the Distinguished Service Medal. The citation noted "the first-hand experience acquired in accompanying the 101st Airborne Division in the invasion of Normandy," experience which led to "important modifications in policies and procedures" of the CAD. The citation also noted Mickey's role in the "negotiation and drafting of the Italian Surrender Instrument, the Instrument of Unconditional Surrender of Germany, and the international machinery to be used for the control of Germany after her total defeat." (Mickey was also awarded the Bronze Star, the Army Commendation Ribbon, and other decorations; he was three times nominated for the Legion of Merit and six times for the rank of brigadier general.)

Mickey arrived in occupied Germany a few days after the liberation of the nightmarish concentration camp at Dachau. Mickey took a tour of the camp—the mountains of unburied dead were still there—and was so shocked that his faith in God was momentarily shaken. Mickey, the Jew from New York, wept at what had been done to his Jewish brethren. What he saw must have strongly awakened his sense of historical heritage; this terrible experience would shape the future course of Mickey Marcus's life.

One of Mickey's tasks in Germany was to assist the thousands of displaced persons. Mickey, however, also had a significant role in making Allied policy for conquered Germany. As Executive for Internal Affairs, then Acting Chief of Staff of the U.S. Group Control Council, and then U.S. Secretary-General in occupied Berlin, Mickey was in effect the number three American in on-site determination of occupation policy. Mickey did not favor policies that would level Germany and reduce it to an agricultural state. To do this would make Germany a virtual slave state dependent on American aid and a country where resentments would eventually boil into new troubles. Mickey did favor the uprooting of the military tradition in Germany, which he saw as the main future threat.

After carrying out his tasks in occupied Germany, Mickey still had one more job to do in uniform. He returned to the Pentagon and was made head of its War Crimes Division. His responsibility was to select judges, prosecutors, and lawyers for the major war trials in Germany and Japan. He traveled extensively to accomplish this and then he attended the trials at Nuremberg, where he felt the truth about the Nazis was "thoroughly exposed for future generations to brood upon."

The war was over, the enemy leaders were being meted justice, and in the spring of 1947 Mickey Marcus returned to his wife and civilian life. This hiatus, however, was not to be for long.

In the Mideast, the Jewish population in the Holy Land was struggling to establish the first independent Jewish state in two thousand years. The British were preparing to pull out, and the neighboring Arab states were gearing to take over, expecting to prevent the establishment of a long-feared Jewish country. The Jews had some weapons, they had several clandestine organizations—the main one being the Haganah (Defense Organization)—and they had a number of officers and soldiers who had gained experience fighting in World War II with the British. They also held to a grim determination: to establish an independent fatherland, or die trying. Major military strength, however—weapons, ammunition supply, air power, military organization, staff capabilities—rested overwhelmingly with the Arab countries.

In December, 1947, Mickey, who had entered private law practice, was contacted by Major Shlomo Shamir, representing the "Provisional Jewish Government." Shamir had been sent to the United States to find and recruit an American military expert or experts who could assist the soon-to-be-born Israeli state in shaping the modern army it would need to survive the onslaught of its enemies. Initially Mickey limited himsef to helping Shamir try to recruit a suitable military figure. Nevertheless it was apparent to all concerned—except perhaps Mickey himself—that he was the experienced and knowledgeable soldier, planner, and administrator that Israel desperately needed.

In January Mickey lunched with Shamir and Moshe Sharett, the ranking Jewish emissary in the United States. Sharett pressed Mickey to take up the Israeli cause; Mickey agreed to discuss the matter with his wife. But Emma protested—she did not want to lose her husband to war again. Mickey drew a parallel between Israel and the struggle of the American colonies: "What if everybody had abandoned the colonials? Where would George Washington have been without help—French arms, Haym Solomon's money, Lafayette and Von Steuben and Kościuszko?" Mickey did not consider himself a Zionist, but he had seen Dachau and he had seen the pitiable remnants of the Jewish population of Europe. He felt that here was a vast challenge, and Mickey Marcus thrived on meeting challenges. The assignment also offered the prospect of adventure, danger, and a leadership role that could result in an immensely satisfying reward: helping a whole people to achieve freedom and independence, a people who had been struggling toward that goal for twenty centuries.

Colonel David (Mickey) Marcus in 1948. (Courtesy of Consulate General of Israel in New York.)

Emma could not refuse Mickey his wish.

Late in January, 1948, Mickey flew to Palestine. The situation there for the Jews was extremely grave. The United Nations had voted to partition Palestine into separate Jewish and Arab states on October 1, 1948. Until that date the British would remain in at least nominal control, but since 1945 guerrilla warfare had been waged by the Jews and the Arabs, with the British caught in the middle. The Arabs were determined that an independent Jewish state should not be created.

Mickey knew what he would find when he arrived: the Jews were outgunned, outnumbered, and outstaffed. He wrote his wife: "The task seems so gigantic. No one man can do this job; were there fifty men here trained at staff level, perhaps that would be enough.

"Yet, one has to dig some earth before an Empire State building is erected. I shall think only of the individual cubicles and perhaps an edifice may arise...."

Mickey was impressed by the youths he encountered: "They are physically and mentally a new breed of men. Yes, a different kind of Jew is being born; and if the baby is not to perish, all the help that America can give, must be given NOW."

Mickey, who used the *nom de guerre* "Michael Stone," took a hard firsthand look at the Jewish forces and later reported to David Ben-Gurion, who would soon be Israel's first prime minister. Mickey explained to Ben-Gurion: "The Haganah is an underground force. With the British running the country, it's had to be. It's main job has been to defend the settlements. And to stage a reprisal now and then.... [It is] a body of irregulars operating in small units: companies, platoons, even sections of six and eight men."

Marcus indicated that changes were necessary, because the Jewish forces now confronted a far greater challenge: "What we face now is a very different business. The minute the British pull out in the spring, we're going to be hit on every border by modern professional armies: heavily equipped, numerically superior, and organized for large-scale actions. They've been trained by British and French officers not to make a stab at a village, but to mount a coordinated offensive, along a front of perhaps a hundred miles ... to slice off whole territories and isolate enemy forces."

Mickey's monumental task was to assist the Jews in transforming their irregular forces into a modern army—overnight. He set about his work with his customary dynamism. He traveled hundreds of miles to visit clandestine Haganah bases. He examined troop dispositions, he studied the fighting qualities of the men, he viewed combat training for officers. Mickey made suggestions; he tried to see that frontline troops had the supplies and weapons they needed. His service in the multinational Allied Forces of World War II stood him in good stead: he was diplomatic, and although a foreigner, managed not to offend. As Yigael Yadin, the Haganah chief of operations, stated, "From the moment he burst like a bombshell into our underground headquarters ... we immediately admired, respected—and above all, loved him."

Mickey's interest and counsel ranged from tactical to strategic matters. At a military base in the Jordan Valley he asked the commander, "How do you communicate with your troops?"

"Use the telephone," was the response.

"And if the Arabs cut the lines?"

"Well, the company will repair them."

"What if the Arabs blow up the powerhouse?"

"In that case," said the officer, "I guess we'd have to send out messengers."

A bit taken aback, Mickey told the officer: "Radios are quicker—and safer. I'll see that you get some."

Mickey knew that modern warfare is not a matter of just shooting at your enemy. He stressed the need for Haganah to develop a logistics capability: "[The] Haganah people [must] understand the importance of logistics. Soon the war will spread, the units will grow—and their toughest problems will be not the actual fighting, but supplies."

Mickey had a say in the structuring of a headquarters staff for the Haganah, making suggestions that were incorporated into the final design. For the basic unit of troop organization Mickey favored a 2,500-man brigade, big enough to launch large attacks but not as difficult to command and maneuver as full-sized divisions. Each brigade had its combat force plus its own artillery, supply train, reconnaissance capability, and reserve troops. The brigade was adopted by the Jewish army, and of this change Yitzchak Rabin, an officer who would one day become chief of staff of the Israeli army, later commented, "It resulted in the creation of a powerful assault group—our first experience of a real offensive force. It was precisely this same striking power, later launched against Lydda and Ramleh, that finally broke the back of the Arab Legion."

Mickey toured the Negev Desert and then presciently counseled Ben-Gurion: "The Negev will be your first theater of war. The minor war now being conducted there is for the communications lines. This will continue to be true after the [Arab] invasion; the invading force will have to stick to the roads, since it will be unable to advance otherwise."

Mickey also provided Ben-Gurion with his evaluation of the Jewish fighting man: "At the moment you have groups of barefoot fighters lacking in even the minimum equipment, but anxious to fight nevertheless. Give them shoes and they will fight even better. They pretend to despise training manuals, they put on an act of knowing everything—but teach them, and they take in instruction with surprising speed in spite of their present apparently cynical attitude."

The Jewish forces had no training manual of their own. Mickey had hoped to bring in U.S. Army manuals, but when this was not possible he solved the problem in typical fashion: he himself wrote a detailed manual specifically tailored to the needs of the Jewish troops. Always Mickey stressed aggressive action. In a section on the "Tactical Use of Infantry Battalion and Company" he wrote: "The Battalion Commander has to be aggressive, with the *capacity for acting immediately and decisively.* These attitudes create a feeling of trust in him among his subordinates. By his *courageous, energetic personal behavior* he creates a proper atmosphere among his entire staff."

From writing a manual to helping structure a general staff—Mickey's influence was pervasive. His work in Palestine was interrupted by a return to the States to be with Emma, who had fallen ill, but then he returned. Moshe Sharett had convinced both Mickey and Emma that Mickey's services were indispensable to Israel: "One could almost say, Mickey is the pillar on which the new Haganah is based."

The British, tired of being caught in the crossfire between the Jews and Arabs, weary of trying to maintain peace in a land in which there was no peace, decided to

Colonel Marcus, 1948, in Israel. (Courtesy of Consulate General of Israel in New York.)

Colonel Marcus, 1948, in Israel, enjoying some exercise. (Private collection.)

withdraw their forces on May 15, 1948. On the afternoon of May 14 the independent state of Israel was proclaimed—and Israel was invaded by the forces of Egypt, Iraq, Syria, Lebanon, and Transjordan.

This new, tiny state—its enemies encompassed territories one hundred times as large with apopulation edge of about sixty to one—was now fighting for its life. But fight it did, and well indeed. The war was a classic: a people with few reserve capabilities and little territory to fall back on used judicious offensive actions to maintain a great defense.

Egyptian troops were driving into the Negev, spearheaded by tanks and armored cars and accompanied by heavy artillery. Mickey urged a counterattack: "You'll say we haven't the forces to attack. I say we have. Even with light units we can raid the enemy's military centers before he's had time to get organized—stop him from placing his guns and preparing his armor. We can exploit his fear of night-fighting, jab at his supply lines, keep him off balance. That's the way the American Rangers were trained to fight: to maintain a strategic defensive against superior forces, by constant, harassing local attacks!"

Ben-Gurion listened and dispatched a unit equipped with newly received machine guns and radio-equipped jeeps to the Negev. Mickey was sent with the detachment in a supervisory position; formal command was entrusted to an Israeli officer. The unit slashed through the Negev, harassing the Egyptians, and Mickey happily found himself in combat again. He related one incident to a war correspondent:

"We knew the Arabs had a dozen good machine guns on this hill. It was suicide with what we had….

"I put a few kids with two-inch mortars at strategic spots covering three sides of the hill. We managed to ease up close without being spotted. I had the mortars open up—they make a hell of a noise, you know. Well, they turned their machine guns on the mortars—but I had my main force run up the fourth side of the hill … and before the Arabs knew what in hell was going on, we were on top of them.

"We took twelve machine guns intact."

Fighting tenaciously, the Israelis brought the invasion to a halt, and in some areas even hurled the enemy back beyond the original frontiers of Palestine. Among the bitterest fighting was that for control of the city of Jerusalem, which Israel had designated to be its capital. Of lesser military importance, the city was of enormous spiritual value: it is the holy city of the Christian, Hebrew, and Islamic faiths. Sections of the city were inhabited by Jews, other parts by Arabs. The result: the streets were strewn with rubble and barricades, the fighting was house by house and block by block. The Jordanian Arab Legion was thrown into the struggle for the city. This elite six thousand-man Bedouin force had been trained and was led by British officers. The commander was a famed British soldier of fortune, Major General John Bagot Glubb (he became a pasha and was well known as "General Glubb Pasha," which did not lessen his fighting abilities a bit).

The Legion and other Arab forces virtually encircled Jerusalem, placing the Jewish sectors under siege and laying down a continuing artillery barrage. Near a village named Latrun, the Legion succeeded in cutting the vital highway link between Jerusalem and Tel Aviv and the coast. Latrun lay near rugged terrain which provided natural defenses, and these were supplemented by manmade defenses including a thick-walled police station built by the British Army.

The Jews were determined to hold on to Jerusalem; the Arabs were determined to conquer it. Their supply line cut, the Arab Legion pressing in, suffering daily cannonading, the Jews in Jerusalem were in a critical position. It became even more critical when an Israeli attempt to capture Latrun was defeated, and then a Jewish-held section of Jerusalem known as the Old City fell to the Arabs.

Not only were the Israelis defending Jerusalem lacking in weapons, supplies, and trained fighters, there was also no single command in charge of the defense of the city. There was even rivalry between the various Israeli units: the Haganah's Etzioni Brigade, inside the city, and 7th Brigade, outside Jerusalem; the Har-EI Brigade (outside) of the Palmach, a semiautonomous branch of the Haganah; and the men and women of the Irgun Tsvai Leumi (National Military Organization), which had formerly been a clandestine terrorist organization. (The leader of the Irgun was a Polish intellectual named Menachem Begin, who as prime minister of Israel would thirty-one years later sign Israel's first peace treaty with Egypt.)

A unified command was essential if Jerusalem was to be saved. Ben-Gurion and the other leaders decided there was one man who combined the military ability with the diplomatic capability needed if the Israeli forces were to be welded together and used to their full potential. On May 28, 1948 the following order was issued by Ben-Gurion:

> Brigadier General Stone [Marcus's *nom de guerre*] is hereby appointed Commander of the Jerusalem Front, with command over the Etzioni, Har-EI, and Seventh Brigades. General Stone is authorized to select officers and noncoms from the aforementioned three brigades to form his staff.

It was a historic moment: Mickey Marcus had achieved the rank of brigadier general. He had been given his first field command, and it was an extraordinarily important one at that. He was the first Jew to command what amounted to an army division. He was, in fact, the highest ranking Jewish battle commander since the Maccabeuses of the second century before Christ.

And there was this ironic footnote to history: an American soldier of fortune was now in command of troops fighting troops led by a British soldier of fortune, and the result of their confrontation would affect the future of a whole new nation.

Mickey saw as his top priority the capture of Latrun and the reopening of the highway to Jerusalem. Plans were drawn up, preparations were made, and in the early hours of May 31 the attack was launched. Although the actual assault was under the command of Mickey's old friend Shlomo Shamir, Mickey went up to the front area with his troops to keep a close eye on developments. The Israelis made initial gains but the Arab legionnaires fought hard and utilized their superior artillery—"It's as bad as the Normandy beaches," Mickey commented as he watched the battle unfold. An Israeli battalion was supposed to come up and descend on the Arabs from the rear, but it encountered heavy resistance and failed to complete its maneuver. The Israeli attack was beaten back. The road to Jerusalem remained closed.

Was there any other way to get supplies to the beleaguered city? There had been instances when men and vehicles had been able to traverse a dirt road through a wadi south of the highway. Mickey sent out a small reconnaissance party. Based on its report, and after a staff discussion, he decided upon a project to make the crude route passable for the trucks needed to get supplies into Jerusalem.

Mickey sent a message to Ben-Gurion and then followed it with a personal visit. The Israeli leader concurred with the plan. Soldiers began work on the road. Bulldozers, civilian laborers, and skilled stonecutters were brought in. Mickey was building Israel's version of the World War II Burma Road. It was essential that construction of the road be kept secret, or else an Arab lunge or artillery might destroy it. In some areas the Arabs were less than five hundred yards away. Most of the work was done at night. Outposts were set up along the route to keep enemy observers away; troops provided protection for the unarmed workers. Mickey supervised the work, constantly riding his jeep along the growing route to see firsthand how it was progressing.

Even before the road was completed Mickey managed to take into Jerusalem a jeep convoy bearing desperately needed mortars, four four-inch weapons. These would boost not only the strained Jewish defenses, but also the morale of the defenders. When the weapons made it into the city, the joyous citizenry hugged and kissed the jeep drivers and the artillerymen. For Mickey it was a most rewarding sight.

Another assault on Latrun was mounted. This one also failed. It did not matter much, however: the "Marcus Road"—as some people were calling it—was now open and supplies were flowing into Jerusalem. The siege had been lifted. It had been raised and the city saved, not by a counterattack but by the building of a road. An Israeli monument to the road would later express gratitude to "our commander Mickey Marcus who came to us from afar, a fighting man who knew the souls of men."

Jerusalem—or at least the modern portion of it—had been preserved for Israel, and the Arab attack had been largely beaten back. A mediator representing the United Nations, Count Folke Bernadotte, negotiated a truce which was to go into effect at 10:00 A.M. (Israeli time) on June 11, 1948.

The village of Abu Ghosh lies some eight miles east of Jerusalem. It was in Israeli hands, as was the nearby Monastère Notre Dame de la Nouvelle Alliance, taken over by the Palmach as a rear headquarters after Benedictine monks moved out due to close-by artillery bombardment. It was to this monastery, set atop a hill, that Mickey came to wait for the truce but at the same time to prepare for the eventuality that fighting might not end. Mickey's continuing concern was that the secret road might be discovered and attacked. He was considering still another attack on Latrun.

The day before the ceasefire was to go into effect, Mickey visited the troops in their tents, took care of administrative matters, called for air support for an Israeli detachment that was under last-minute Arab attack, and sent reinforcements to block a second Arab strike. He issued an order of the day on the subject of honesty among soldiers and, probably recalling his Torah studies, stated, "The Jewish Army is based on the highest ethical and moral principles!" That night there was a party to celebrate the upcoming truce.

It was after midnight when Mickey retired to his room. Restless and not sleeping, in the early morning hours he slipped out of the building. A sentry saw him, knew who he was, waved him on.

The time was 3:35 A.M. Shortly, a relief soldier took over from the sentry.

Soon afterwards the relief man heard trampling noises in the bush and then dimly spotted a figure moving. "Who goes there?" he called out in Hebrew.

He heard an indistinct answer.

The soldier, aware that he was guarding a military headquarters, fired a warning shot in the air.

The figure kept advancing. One hand was held upward—with a greeting or a grenade?

The sentry fired once.

By the time they reached him, Mickey Marcus lay dead with an Israeli bullet in his heart. He was the last Israeli fatality prior to the truce.

Military funeral of David Marcus, West Point class of 1924, on July 1, 1948. (Courtesy of the U.S. Military Academy Archives.)

David Ben-Gurion placing a wreath on David "Mickey" Marcus's grave. (Courtesy of U.S. Military Academy Archives.)

Before leaving for Palestine on his last trip, Mickey had promised his wife that he would be "back in June." A United States transport plane bore Mickey back to his homeland on June 30, his casket draped in an Israeli flag. This was then replaced with the Stars and Stripes, and an honor guard of New York policemen saluted as the casket was lowered from the plane. There were services at Union Temple in Brooklyn, and then Mayor William O'Dwyer led observances at City Hall.

And finally, burial took place at the cemetery at West Point, attended by American and Israeli civilians, including Maxwell Taylor, who had helped lead the United States to victory in World War II, and Moshe Dayan, who would lead Israel to victory in a later war. Emma was there, saying her last farewell.

When he was laid to rest, Mickey was the only West Pointer, of the more than three thousand soldiers buried in that cemetery, to have been killed fighting under a foreign flag.

The gravestone says: "Colonel David Marcus—A Soldier for All Humanity."

David Ben-Gurion put it thus: "He was the best man we had."

CHAPTER 4

The French Foreign Legion: A Tradition of Courage

Beau Geste: "With a hundred rounds of ammunition in our pouches, joy in our hearts, and a terrific load upon our backs, we swung out of the gates to the music of our magnificent band, playing the March of the Legion, never heard save when the Legion goes on active service. Where we were going, we neither knew nor cared. That it would be a gruelling murderous march, we knew and did not care."

The fictional Legion sergeant in another novel, telling his recruits not to try to desert: "If you leave, the desert will get you, and if the desert doesn't get you, the Arabs will get you and if the Arabs don't get you, I will get you."

And the real-life General François de Negrier telling the Legionnaires arriving in Haiphong, Indochina, in 1883: "You legionnaires are soldiers in order to die, and I am sending you where you can die."

White kepis aslant, heavy loads on backs, sun-drenched dunes, white forts flying the tricolor, thirst, cruel discipline, endless treks, sudden skirmishes, pain, bloody tunics, capture, torture, heroes, heroines, heroism—clear visions conjured up by the mere name, "French Foreign Legion." Probably no fighting group in history is better known than the Legion—it is the stuff of which great romances are dreamed and created, the pinnacle of Fighting Man. The legends of the Legion are legend. And many of them are real, too.

On March 9, 1831, King Louis-Philippe established "a legion of foreigners to be known as the Foreign Legion for service outside France." It was a period of severe turbulence in France and throughout Europe. Frustrated revolutionaries from other countries found shelter in Paris, and so did unsuccessful mercenaries. But there was hunger and unemployment and just plain unruliness and social dissatisfaction. Paris was wracked by riots and looting. Amid the chaos the French government had its eye on building an empire in North Africa. When the war minister came up with the idea for the Legion, King Philippe acquiesced and the Legion was formed. The intent was to harness the energies of the malcontents and put them to work, building an empire on the sand dunes of North Africa.

The Legion, at first, was little more than a work battalion. When it was thrown into combat with the Berbers, the legionnaires fled ignominiously. They were, nevertheless, soon to receive their first opportunity to fight in another land. In 1834 a revolution broke out against the government of Spain because a royal heir, Carlos, felt that he had been unfairly deprived of his right to the throne. France, England, and Portugal decided to support the reigning Spanish government. England sent a mercenary group of 9,600 men known as the "Spanish Legion." And France, as its contribution, rented its Foreign Legion to the Spanish government. There followed five years of warfare. The French Legion proved to be the backbone of the government forces. It particularly distinguished itself at the battles of Terapegui (1836) and Huesca (1837). The revolt was finally suppressed, and Carlos took refuge in France. The Legion left Spain in January, 1839, by then having lost fifty percent of its initial strength. But it had proved its fighting worth.

In Africa, France was trying to build an empire. France in 1830 had invaded Algeria; seven years later that country had still not been pacified. Abd el-Kader, a young—in his twenties—Berber warrior, had inflicted the defeat on the Legion in 1835. In the following years he proved himself a skillful general, leading the Algerian mountain tribes against the French infidel. Today he would be termed a religious fanatic. Wherever he went, the Koran and Islamic teachings went with him.

For a year the mountain citadel city of Constantine, manned by Turks and Kabyle tribesmen, held out against attacks by French forces. In October, 1837, some twenty thousand French troops gathered for a new assault on the Islamic bastion. For five days the citadel was subjected to artillery bombardment. Finally, when a sufficiently large breach had been blasted through a wall, a French officer, son of King Philippe, signalled with his white lace handkerchief. Legionnaires charged forward, scrambling over the rubble of the wall, driving through the fire of the Turks and Kabyles. A Legion colonel was hit by two musket balls. He headed slowly back to the French lines. The king's son asked, "How goes the assault?" The colonel gave a report. "But you, colonel, you're wounded," exclaimed the prince. *"Non, monseigneur,"* responded the Legion officer, "I am dead." He died the following day.

The Legion cracked the defenses of the fortress city. Its men penetrated the hole in the wall and swept on into the streets and alleys of Constantine. Other French troops followed. Two hours later the city was in the hands of the French. (The commander of the French army, Marshal C.M.D. Damremont, died in the assault.)

Abd el-Kader had previously signed a peace treaty with the French, but with the taking of Constantine he claimed that the agreement had been broken. He took to the field again with a well-trained force of two thousand cavalry, eight thousand infantry, and some fifty thousand irregular horse soldiers. He seized towns, raided French garrisons, even approached the capital at Algiers. In June, 1840 a French column, which included one infantry and one Legion battalion, entered the town of Miliaria, which had been razed by Arabs. The French began rebuilding, but soon Abd el-Kader raided the town and placed it under siege. The defenders' food supplies were consumed and had to be strictly rationed. Heat and disease took an increasingly heavy toll. When Abd el-Kader staged an attack in August, no more than four hundred soldiers could rise in defense of the fort protecting the city. Men went insane, believing that black beetles had entered their bodies and were gnawing at their brains.

Then one day a legionnaire who had deserted or been captured entered the garrison with his wife. He offered to take a message to the French headquarters in Algiers, seventy miles away. The offer was accepted. Not until almost two months later, however, did a relief column reach the garrison. Eight hundred men had died; three hundred were seriously ill. Only one hundred men were able to march out. Another chapter of valor was written in the history of the Legion.

The French government sent Marshal Thomas R. Bugeaud to complete the pacification of North Africa. Combining and putting to work his fine military and administrative qualities, Bugeaud established a few fixed bases and from these sent flying columns to fight the Berbers. The Berbers had been highly mobile. Now the French were also. Bugeaud ordered the Legion into lightweight, more functional uniforms and taught it to adopt Abd el-Kader tactics, striking rapidly, seizing livestock, burning crops. New towns were built as well as roads to connect them. Outposts provided protection. Bugeaud added indigenous units to the French army and established a combat assault formation which he called the "boar's head." The programs and policies initiated by Bugeaud would serve as the guidelines for the French rulers in North Africa for a century.

As for Abd el-Kader, things did not go well with him. At Smala a French flying column attacked the Berber leader's much larger army, defeated it, and sent it fleeing. Systematically Abd el-Kader was forced toward Morocco and then into that country. Marshall Bugeaud pursued him with 6,000 infantry, 1,500 cavalry, and some artillery. Abd el-Kader camped with 45,000 men by the Isly River. Bugeaud, in relentless pursuit, crossed the river and attacked. His "boar's head" formations repulsed Berber assaults, and then his cavalry—the "boar's tusks"—counterattacked and overran the Berber camp. Some minor fighting continued in the years ahead but finally in December, 1847, Abd el-Kader surrendered to the French. He was imprisoned for several years and then released. He is viewed today not only as a great general but also a fine scholar. For the Legion, he had been a hard and wily foe for a dozen years.

The year was 1854. A jurisdictional squabble over holy places in Jerusalem had escalated into a major European conflict. France and England, acting in support of Turkey, went to war with Russia. A French and English expeditionary force—52,000 men in 150 ships—sailed to the Black Sea and landed at the town of Varna, in Bulgaria, and then moved on to stage another landing on the Crimean Peninsula, The goal was to capture the strategic Russian naval base at Sevastopol. The entire campaign had been marked by muddling and dissension among the French and British commanders, to say nothing of cholera, which swept through the allied expedition. Nevertheless, the allied troops did manage to get ashore, and this without having to do any fighting. The Russians, too, were hardly conducting a brilliant military campaign and had managed to concentrate their troops in the wrong zones.

The Russian commander, Prince Alexander Menshikov, decided to make his defense along the banks of the Alma River. The allies crossed the river, but the British found themselves fighting hard to gain a steep slope on the other side. One of the French commanders, General Certain Canrobert, a former Legionnaire, was hit by a cannonball but survived. The French forces ran forward in a disorganized manner, and then the Legion appeared—hardened, disciplined troops marching as if on parade. "Ah," said Canrobert, "my brave Legionnaires. Set the others an example at the right moment." The Legionnaires drove into the Russian lines and then held the ground they had captured. There was more bitter fighting, and at last Menshikov withdrew his army. The allied position was secured.

The siege of Sevastopol would go on for a full year, marked by a bitter winter (during which Legionnaires killed and skinned a British billy goat mascot), the ministrations of Florence Nightingale, the magnificent and useless charge of the British Light Cavalry Brigade, and what was probably the first battle appearance of ironclad warships (three iron-plated French floating batteries that bombarded the Russians). On September 9, 1855, the port city finally fell to the allies.

For the Legion it was back to Sidi bel-Abbes, its famed headquarters post, back to the hot sands of North Africa, so preferable to the ruthless winter of Russia. And then another country, another war.

France had decided to try to dislodge the Austrians who occupied Italy, and the Legion would be part of the attacking French force. Early in June, 1859, French troops were marching through Lombardy, and on the fourth of the month they encountered and fought the Austrians near the town of Magenta. A French flank crumpled. Only two Legion battalions in the region stood firm. The Legion commander, Colonel Granet Lacroix de Chabriere, ordered: "No retreat! Keep the sunny side of them. Down sacks and charge." The colonel was hit in the chest by a bullet, knocking him off his horse. A sergeant rushed to him. Colonel Chabriere sat up and said: "I must tell you something. *Vive la Legion!*" And he was dead. Of such fabric are legends made.

The Legionnaires battled their way into Magenta, the first French troops to enter the city. Other Frenchmen followed and the city was taken. The Legionnaires overcelebrated by sacking the city's shops and looting wine cellars. When the Legion's *Boudin* call was bugled, the men refused to respond. Some were found floating dead in wine vats. At Solferino another battle was waged; the Legion again distinguished itself. The Austrians were routed. The following month, July, 1859, the warring sides reached an agreement in which each won points. Like so many other conflicts, this had been an inconclusive war.

Napoleon III was soon ready to embark on another adventure, and this one would take the Legion very far from Sidi bel-Abbes indeed....

Napoleon III dreamed of creating a vast empire in the Western Hemisphere, and as a first step he planned to install Archduke Maximilian, younger brother of Austrian Emperor Francis Joseph, as emperor of Mexico. The Mexican population was not particularly pleased at this prospect, so increasing numbers of French troops had to be dispatched to prepare for Maximilian's installation on the Mexican throne in the name of France. (In those days royal figures got away with playing Monopoly with entire countries.) Among the French military units were three battalions of the Foreign Legion, and they landed in Vera Cruz in March, 1863.

At this time a French army was besieging the town of Puebla, whose strategic location protected the capital, Mexico City. Late in April the French learned that a Mexican unit was planning to seize a wagon train bringing supplies, ammunition, and a considerable quantity of gold from Vera Cruz to the French siege force. The Third Company of the First Battalion of the Legion was sent to meet and protect the wagons. The company consisted of three officers and sixty-two men (and two mules). The commander was Captain Jean Danjou, a veteran of the Legion's wars. He was distinguished by the fact that a wooden hand had replaced one of his hands that had been blown away by an exploding signal pistol. History was about to be made, and this wooden hand would play a part in it.

A Legionnaire in Mexico, 1866. (Courtesy of French Embassy Press and Information Division.)

Captain Jean Danjou, a Legionnaire who had lost a hand in the Crimean campaign, led his troops in the heroic defense of Camerone, where he fell on April 30, 1863. (Courtesy of French Embassy Press and Information Division.)

The relic of the wooden hand of Captain Danjou, which is honored as a symbol of courage in an annual Legion ceremony. (Courtesy of French Embassy Press and Information Division.)

The Legionnaires trekked through the rugged Mexican countryside, and then at a spot called Camerone, they were attacked by Mexican cavalry. The Legionnaires threw back two charges and then sought shelter in a ruined hacienda. In the ensuing hours some two thousand Mexican soldiers maintained their assault on the tiny French detachment. Danjou asked each of his men to promise to die rather than surrender. Each made the promise. The mules had been frightened off, taking with them the unit's provisions.

The French had neither food nor water. They were using up their ammunition. The Mexican fire was taking a mounting toll; Danjou died with a bullet in his chest. The Mexicans offered to accept a surrender; a Legionnaire hurled back the epithet emplgyed by General Pierre Cambronne of the Garde Imperial at Waterloo when he was asked to give up: *"Merde!"*

The smoke swirled as the Legionnaires went down one by one. True to their promise to Daniou, they died rather than surrender. Only a handful remained, and these decided upon a final grand, defiant gesture: a charge against the foe. One lieutenant and four men still stood; they had but one cartridge apiece. "Take aim," ordered the lieutenant. "Fire!" These were the final shots. The men rushed forward with their bayonets fixed. One man dropped, then the lieutenant. The last Legionnaires were face to face with the foe. A Mexican officer pushed aside his men's bayonets with his saber and told the French, "Gentlemen, you must surrender."

A Legionnaire responded that they would do so if they could retain their weapons and equipment and the Mexicans would care for the wounded lieutenant.

The three Legionnaires were taken to the Mexican commander, who exclaimed: "What! Is this all that's left of them?"

The officer who had taken the surrender said, "But they are not men, they are demons!"

The Mexicans treated the prisoners well, and eventually the survivors returned to the French army.

A Legion relief column came—too late—to Camerone, and there buried the dead in a mass grave. A Legionnaire detached Danjou's wooden hand from his body—it became the Legion's most precious relic. Every April 30 is Camerone Day to the Legion, marked by a parade and solemn ceremony. Each year, in the ritual at the Legion's headquarters, the hand is borne by a distinguished former Legionnaire and is saluted by the troops, to celebrate the Legionnaires' traditional gallant courage.

The Legion had its revenge in Mexico. General Achille Bazaine, a former Legionnaire who had risen through the ranks, broke the siege of Puebla about a fortnight after Camerone. French troops entered Mexico City early in June and Maximilian was installed on the throne. Bazaine was promoted to overall command of the French forces, and within weeks he had pushed the forces of Mexican leader Benito Juarez into the deserts north of Monterey; Juarez himself sought asylum in the United States.

But with the end of the Civil War, which had been raging in the United States, the U.S. government turned its attention to developments south of the border. The French were told to get out—an order supported by General Phil Sheridan and fifty thousand veteran troops poised on the border. Bazaine evacuated his troops from Mexico, but Maximilian refused to leave. He was captured, court-martialed, and on June 19, 1867, he was executed.

Another decade, another war, another country—this time France itself. Napoleon III had not done well in Italy; he was thrown out of Mexico. Nevertheless, he decided he could take on Bismarck's Prussians and declared war on them on July 15, 1870. The Foreign Legion was actually barred by its charter from serving in France itself, but this war again did not go well for the French. Prussian intelligence had obtained the complete French order of battle; French intelligence, in turn, was almost nonexistent. The French suffered successive defeats, and the Germans advanced deep into France.

Fortunately France is an emotional homeland to more than just French nationals and thousands of foreigners—Belgians, Swiss, English, Americans, Chinese—offered their services. Even Germans living in France offered to fight for France. The foreigners were recruited and a foreign detachment was organized and trained. (Just in case, the German volunteers were sent off to the Legion in Algeria.)

The foreign unit was called into action to defend the French city of Orléans against Bavarian and Prussian troops. The foreigners fought fiercely, house to house, and when finally they were forced to retreat across the Loire River only 180 men out of the original 1,500 could walk, and many of these were wounded. Only one of twenty-two officers remained. Legionnaires were then brought over from Algiers, and they spearheaded a French counterattack at Orléans—and covered the retreat when the assault failed.

The French asked for peace and bowed to Bismarck's reparation and territorial demands. German troops entered Paris, but this proud city refused to surrender and took to the barricades. Over a thousand Legionnaires were sent into the city, and now the Legionnaires were fighting Frenchmen in an effort to restore order for a French government. It took the Legion a week and considerable casualties to pacify the rebellious city. Afterwards, a job of cleaning the streets for the Legionnaires, and then back to Algeria.

During the nineteenth century European powers stretched greedy fingers into Asia, and France was no exception. French attention focused on Indochina. In 1858 an expeditionary force of 15 warships and 1,500 French troops, plus 850 Filipino troops provided by France's ally Spain, attacked and captured the port of Tourane (now Da Nang). The French conquest destined to have vast historical consequences was underway. First the southern portions of Indochina in a were annexed, then the French turned north. When the French moved into the Tonkin region adjoining China, the Chinese objected and war resulted. And the Legion was there, walking

Legion drummers forming up, date uncertain. (Courtesy of French Embassy Press and Information Division.)

through the wet paddy fields and suffering the jungle, as it would for another seventy-five years. The French laid siege to Son Tay fortress but were unable to breach the walls. A Legion sapper, wielding only his ax, leapt a moat and made his way through a breach blown by artillery. He seized a banner from the Chinese and, being Belgian, yelled: "Long live Belgium! Long live the Legion!" Legionnaires, rushing forward with their bayonets, routed the Chinese.

The years went by and the Legion marched and fought on: more battles with the Chinese in Indochina. A campaign to oust Behanzin, the "Shark King" of Dahomey, Africa, whose army included a force of ruthless amazons. The conquest of Madagascar.

And then came the big one—the first of what would be known as the world wars. Again the Legion would fight within France itself. At the outset of the conflict, the Legion numbered some eight thousand men. During the four years of war more than thirty-six thousand men from over fifty countries joined the famed elite corps. By the time of the armistice in November, 1918, Legion casualties included thirty-one thousand dead, missing, and presumed dead. During this war, the Legion wrote a large page in its history, and it was a page writ with blood and bravery: Vimy Ridge, Champagne, the Somme, Gallipoli, Belloy-en-Santerre, the Marne.

The Legion on parade in North Africa in a half-track. (Courtesy of French Embassy and Information Division.)

A patrol of Legionnaires leaving a fort in North Africa on a reconnaissance, after hearing of rebel movement in the area. (Courtesy of French Embassy Press and Information Division.)

In February, 1916, the city of Verdun had been placed under siege by the Germans, and Marshal Henri Petain declared, "They shall not pass!" The siege lasted throughout most of the year. When the Germans withdrew fifteen divisions for an offensive on the Russian front, Petain decided to try to break out. A Legion attack was ordered, and Petain and General John Pershing, a commander of the American forces in France, watched as the Legionnaires moved forward in early morning. They captured their initial objective within hours and kept going, fighting through the night. "Where are you exactly? Why have you moved beyond your objectives?" The Legion colonel wrote his reply: "You have given the Legion too limited an objective. It has assigned itself others."

Americans joined up to fight for France—or just to fight. War had broken out in August, 1914, and that month some seventy Americans signed up with the Legion. More joined as the war progressed. They were a mixed group—a typical Legion lot: Bob Scanlon, a black boxer; Hendrik van Loon, who would become an important historian; Ivan Nock, a mining engineer; Harry Collins, a sailor; Robert Percy, another boxer; brothers Kiffin and Paul Rockwell—Kiffin later joined the Lafayette Squadron; Jules Bach, engineer; Siegfried Narvitz, philosophy professor; Edmond Genet, descendant of the Genet of French Revolution fame.

Dr. David Wheeler had been a prominent surgeon in Buffalo, New York; he volunteered to work in a French Red Cross hospital. But he found treating the wounded too depressing; he sought excitement and decided the best way to find it was in the Legion. At the age of forty-two he joined the Legion and found his war. He fought well and bravely—a soldier, not a surgeon. At a place called Navarin Farm, Wheeler and a buddy, an Englishman cashiered from his country's army who had then joined the Legion, were wounded and fell together. "Old fellow, I'm afraid they'll have to take that off," Wheeler told the other Legionnaire, whose right leg had been incapacitated by bullets. Although wounded himself, Wheeler tended his buddy. After treating his own wound he fainted. The two lay in a trench for hours before being rescued. When the United States entered the war, Wheeler joined the American fighting forces and was killed a few months before the armistice.

The best-known American in the Legion was noted for a talent not generally attributed to a Legionnaire: he was a writer of poetry. Thin, soulful Alan Seeger arrived in Paris in 1912 to compose poetry, and he had just published his first book of verse when war broke out. To defend *la belle France,* he joined the Legion. In his diary he wrote: "I have joined up in order that France, and especially Paris, which I love, should never cease to be the glory and beauty which they are." Initially at least, Seeger was far better with a pen than with a rifle. The German corporal in charge of Seeger's unit asked him where he had learned to mishandle a weapon the way he did. Seeger lied: in the Mexican army, he said. "Not eefen the Mexican army is so clumsy," harrumphed the German.

In June, 1916, the American Legionnaires were planning to spend July 4 in Paris on leave, but it was not to be so. A major Allied offensive was in the offing, and the Legion would be part of it. Seeger, by now a lieutenant, wrote home, "We go up to the attack tomorrow. This will probably be the biggest thing yet. We are to have the honor of marching in the first wave.... I am glad to be going in the first wave. If you are in this thing at all, it is best to be in to the limit. And this is the supreme experience."

The objective was Belloy-en-Santerre, a village that the Germans had turned into a bulwark. Seeger led his men through heavy German fire and up a slope. A friend later reported, "I caught sight of Seeger and called to him, making a sign with my hand. He answered with a smile. His tall silhouette stood out.... His head erect and pride in his eye, I saw him running forward with his bayonet fixed. Soon he disappeared and that was the last I saw my friend."

A bullet struck Seeger in the stomach and he fell into a trench. He was heard calling for water and for his mother.

Later, a burial party would find a naked body—someone had stripped it—and the dogtag number, 195522, would identify what was left of Alan Seeger. He was buried on the spot. Once he had presciently written:

> I have a rendezvous with Death
> At some disputed barricade,
> When Spring comes back with rustling shade
> And apple-blossoms fill the air—
>
> ...I've a rendezvous with Death
> At midnight in some flaming town,
> When Spring trips north again this year,
> And I to my pledged word am true,
> I shall not fail that rendezvous.

Belloy-en-Santerre was taken, but the cost was the lives of 1,200 Legionnaires.

Between the great wars the Foreign Legion kept the tricolor aloft in the colonies and maintained France's authority over the colonials. The major campaign of this period was fought in Morocco, which the European powers insisted on treating the way they treated parts of Asia. Local tribes objected to this and took up arms. France and Spain had split Morocco between them as colonies, and for most of the first three decades of the twentieth century, French and Spanish forces were employed in trying to convince the Moroccan natives of the benefits of European rule.

Unrest spread through much of Spanish Morocco. The Spaniards succeeded in pacifying the western region of the country, but in the east, Abdel Krim, a canny chieftain of the Riffian tribe, led his forces to victory, destroying a twenty thousand-man Spanish army. Krim now turned his attention to French Morocco, sweeping forward in April, 1925 to overwhelm forty-three of sixty-six border outposts, all manned by the Legion. The Legion moved virtually all of its twenty-five thousand men to fight Krim. Krim, however, commanded some one hundred thousand Riffians armed with weapons captured from the Spaniards. Most galling to the Legion was the fact that one of the Riff leader's chief aides was a Legion deserter—former Sergeant Joseph Klems—who taught the Riffs how to handle the artillery they had taken. (He would later be the subject of Sigmund Romberg's romantic operetta, *The Desert Song*.)

France and Spain decided upon a joint offensive, and both nations sent sizable expeditionary forces to fight the Riffs. Marshal Petain, hero of Verdun, commanded the French forces. The Riffs were squeezed between the Spanish forces moving south and the French driving north. Krim surrendered on May 26, 1926, and the Riff War was over. Krim was sent into exile. Klems was captured months later—he had hidden in a mountain cave. "You fought a good fight, Klems," said the Legion officer who captured him. "The Legion respects you."

The years passed, the Legion manned its forts, marched, thirsted, caroused, and maintained the French flag over the desert sands. And then came another great war.

For a while, it appeared that the Legion might not do much fighting. Nazi intelligence had infiltrated it, and the French government was leery of sending its units into action against the German army (the Spanish Civil War had taught the fearful meaning of the words "fifth column"). Instead, three "foreign" regiments were raised inside France, to be trained and led by Foreign Legion officers and noncommissioned officers. These units were sent into the Maginot Line.

When the regular units of the Legion finally did see action, it was in a most unlikely spot: the frozen north. Initially the Legionnaires were to be part of an Anglo-French expedition that was to aid the Finns in their struggle with Russia. Events, however, moved swiftly: Finland came to peace with Russia and Germany invaded Denmark and Norway. The Legion was sent to participate in the taking of the key Norwegian port of Narvik. The German hatred of the Legion dated back to World War I, and when the German commander at Narvik, General Edouard Dietl, learned of the Legion presence he exclaimed: "The Alpine Chasseurs, that's fine. But the Foreign Legion—those international thugs. The British should be ashamed to use them against us."

The "international thugs," although accustomed to desert fighting, nevertheless helped take Narvik and chased crack German mountain troops almost to the border of Sweden. This was to be France's sole victory in the early years of the war.

Already the Nazi juggernaut was rolling through France, Belgium, Luxembourg, and the Netherlands. The Norwegian campaign was abandoned and the Legionnaires were ordered back to France. Encamped near Brest, the Legion prepared to fight. When a young French officer urged the commander of the Legion detachment to surrender and not "cause trouble for us," the Legion colonel shot him dead on the spot. While other French units crumpled, the Legion regiments in the Maginot Line fought on. Underweaponed, undertrained, these men, imbued with the Legion doctrine of death before surrender, stood up against the German tanks, Stukas, and artillery. "Why fight?" asked dispirited French *poilus*. "The Legion dies on its feet!" a Belgian Legionnaire replied. The Legionnaires beat back fierce German assaults, and when these subsided, they counterattacked. A diminishing number kept ahead of the grinding German advance; several hundred eventually managed to get back to Africa.

Other Legionnaires made it to England, where they were reviewed by a French brigadier who had emerged as the rallying point for those Frenchmen who wanted to continue fighting the Nazis: Charles de Gaulle. Those Legionnaires who wished to return to Africa were permitted to do so. All Gaul was divided now, and so was the Legion: some served as Free French; others were under the banner of Vichy. The division would become even more tragic when the two camps, each honoring the flag of France, would face each other as the Allies moved to conquer Syria. The Vichy Legionnaires presented arms to their brothers, buglers on both sides played the *Boudin*, and a bloody battle was on. On June 21, thirteen days after the invasion of Syria began, Damascus was taken, and three weeks later the Vichy commander surrendered. The Legion had helped win another victory, but the Legion—the Vichy Legion—lost, too. Such are the ironies of war.

The Legion, structured as the 13th Demi-Brigade, went on to other victories as part of the Allied forces. It did more than its share in raising anew the prestige of the French Army after the fall of France. The Legion helped the British take the Sudan and Eritrea from the Italians. It stood firm at Bir Hacheim in Libya, blocking a drive on Tobruk by the mighty Erwin Rommel. The Legion fought at EI Alamein and in Tunisia; it fought in Italy. And then came a glorious day—August 16, 1944—when the Legion landed in southern France, returning the tricolor at last to defend its homeland. When France was finally liberated, the Legion was there; it had vindicated the honor of French arms.

For the next seventeen years, however, the Legion fought a losing battle to maintain French sovereignty in two vital areas of the crumbling French empire: Indochina and Algeria. The Japanese had occupied Indochina, but with the Japanese defeat in 1945, France wanted Indochina back. British troops arrived in Saigon on September 12, 1945 and released and armed imprisoned French paratroops. The French seized the city, and eventually as additional French troops, including a sizable portion of the Legion, were brought in, all of Indochina was returned to French control.

The time for colonies was passing, however, and Vietnamese communists and nationalists—Vietnam was a part of Indochina—wanted independence for their country. Negotiations were conducted, and in March, 1946 an agreement was signed in which France recognized Vietnam as "an independent state" but within "the French Union." The agreement was a temporary palliative for a restive situation. Trouble was not long in coming, and there were skirmishes and street fighting. In November, 1946, shooting broke out in the port of Haiphong, and French ships bombarded the city.

Soon full-scale warfare was under way. This was a war that would last eight years and cost the French thirty-five thousand killed and forty-eight thousand wounded. And, again, there was the Legion, plodding through the paddy fields, manning the forts, fighting off ambushes, trying to keep the roads open and the villages controlled. And again the ironies of war: a considerable portion of the Legion was now composed of former German soldiers, recruited in the POW camps in occupied Germany.

The long struggle in Indochina eroded the will to war, particularly in the French homeland. A peace conference was convened in Switzerland in April, 1954, but even as the delegates conferred, the climax and end of the conflict were reached at the heavily fortified town of Dien Bien Phu, besieged by a Vietnamese force under General Vo Nguyen Giap. There, a French garrison of about fifteen thousand men, including almost three thousand Legionnaires, repulsed repeated assaults but was slowly whittled away. The siege lasted fifty-five days and fifty-five nights, and the garrison was all but annihilated. On May 7, 1954, one of the most gallant defenses of modern times ended in surrender.

Halfway around the world, the Algerians also wanted their independence. On May 8, 1954, nationalists clashed with French, leaving eighty-eight Frenchmen and more than one thousand Algerians dead. On November 1, 1954, rebel bands struck over thirty targets, mainly gendarmerie posts in the mountains in the east. The war would draw in one-half of the entire French army, with the Legion now fighting on its home ground. This war also lasted eight years, and it cost the lives of some ten thousand Frenchmen and seventy thousand Algerians.

Growing unrest back home brought General de Gaulle, France's World War II and postwar leader, back to power. De Gaulle, however, instead of cracking down further on the Algerians as expected by the army, offered the Algerians self-determination. A portion of the French army in Algeria rebelled. This included a number of Legionnaires. The 13th Demi-Brigade remained loyal, however; its commander stated, "You'll have to get rid of me before the demi-brigade gets involved in sedition." The revolt was crushed. A ceasefire between the French and Algerians was agreed upon and on July 3, 1962, Algeria became independent.

For the Foreign Legion this was a historic moment; not only had another bitter, bloody conflict come to an end, but now the Legion had to leave Algeria, after 131 years in that country. At Sidi bel-Abbes the Legionnaires packed their belongings, their equipment, their relics—including the wooden hand of Captain Danjou—even their illustrious dead, and moved them to new headquarters at Camp de la Demande at Aubagne, near Marseille. On October 24, 1962, the last Legion parade was held at Sidi bel-Abbes.

Today the Legion lives and fights on. No longer based in Africa, the corps nevertheless continues to serve France on that troubled continent. In the past few years Legionnaires have been involved in supporting a number of France's allies, notably in helping to repel the 1978 invasion of Zaire by Shaba rebels. Thus the Legion-borne tricolor continues to fly in Africa, and Legionnaires still march and die there.

CHAPTER 5

William Brooks: The Legion Today

In the almost one hundred fifty years since the French Foreign Legion was founded, hundreds of American soldiers of fortune have served in it. One of these was William Brooks. From 1963 to 1966, Brooks served in the U.S. 82nd Airborne Division. As an artillery fire direction controller he saw action in Thailand, Vietnam, and the Dominican Republic, where he was wounded.

He joined the Foreign Legion in 1972. This is his story as he told it to author Brown.

The Rue d'Arras is probably the smallest street in Paris. Its only hotel is cheap and full of American students wasting their parents' money at the Sorbonne. It was here, in the Hotel Vendome, that Brooks decided to join the Legion. The Portuguese military attaché had turned him down flat when he asked for work. The Portuguese were (then) winning their wars, he had said. The same was true at the South African embassy. Events in Africa were soon to change, but Brooks was in a hurry. He was going broke and getting bored.

The French Foreign Legion had been in the back of his mind ever since he had decided to leave a secure teaching position and come to Europe. Now the time had come. The lure of the unknown had always been a peculiar motivation for Brooks.

He arrived at Fort de Nogent, Paris, early on Sunday morning, January 23, 1972. A Legionnaire on guard asked, in German, what he wanted. He replied in broken German that he couldn't speak any French, and had come to volunteer. The sergeant of the guard ordered him to wait in a small room while he telephoned the duty officer. A few moments later, a senior noncom, wearing the rank of adjutant (master sergeant) told Brooks to empty his pockets, whereupon he took everything Brooks owned, including money and passport, and placed it in a large envelope. Brooks followed the noncom across the courtyard and up the stairs past a door into a dingy squad bay. The place was dirty, looking more like a skid-row flophouse than a military barracks, but the food was hot and good. Brooks ended his first day in the Legion lying on a cot with a full stomach, watching television.

Every Legionnaire is given an alias. This alias is mandatory for three years. After this time one may request resumption of one's real identity. Whether or not the real identity is returned depends upon the person's police record in civilian life. The name is changed in order to separate the Legionnaire from his past and to protect him from persons seeking his whereabouts. In this way the Legion Security Office effectively discourages anyone seeking to locate a Legionnaire for any reason. A volunteer has all his identity papers confiscated. They are all returned at the end of his five-year enlistment. Every Legionnaire starts anew; what one did before matters only in its relationship to one's being a good Legionnaire. Who one really is, where he came from, and why he joined the Legion are recorded and filed with the Legion's Security Bureau. This file is open only to the Bureau and its contents are kept in strict secrecy.

Brooks signed the contract for the minimum enlistment term of five years. He was given a worn-out World War II uniform, a musette, beret, and ten francs. On Friday evening, January 28, Brooks and a group of about fifty other volunteers under the guidance of an NCO set out by train for Aubagne, a small town east of Marseille and general headquarters of the French Foreign Legion.

In Aubagne are stationed the numerous rear echelon personnel that make any army tick—supply, medical, transit, and music units. The beautiful museum and the white buildings offered an appealing change from dreary, filthy Fort de Nogent, and the appearance of the post lifted Brooks's spirits considerably.

Upon arriving, the EVs (engaged volunteers) were herded into a separate barracks, fenced off by ten-foot-high mesh wire fence that gave one the impression of a prison compound. This is just what it turned out to be. The men were told they would remain there three weeks. During this time they would be given physical and mental tests, issued their clothing allowances, and screened by the Security Bureau.

Everyone was told that if at any time during these weeks he wished to drop out, he would be escorted to the train station and given a ticket to anywhere he wished in France. In other words, the engaged volunteers had three weeks to make up their minds whether they wanted to stay.

During this period everything fell into its regimented place. The men formed into groups depending upon the language spoken. Each group's main objective was trying to avoid work details. Brooks found the confinement suffocating and spent hours on end either reading in bed, standing in line, or pacing back and forth in the exercise yard.

He found some comrades: Peters, an offensive-tackle-sized Finnish seaman, who wanted to try living on land. What Peters lacked in intellectual capabilities he made up for with his arms, his back, and his heart. Matic, the Slav, had only gone as far as eighth grade in school but was a self-taught intellectual who had a working knowledge of ten languages, including old and new Greek.

There was also Brunin, the Irish farm boy and Queen's Irish Guard, whose simple logic, soldierly bearing, and love and knowledge of the Confederate States Army endeared him to Brooks; Penson, the group's translator and French expatriate, had lived ten years in Scotland and was running from an unfaithful wife; Moeller, the son of a World War II German paratrooper, was trying to prove he was as good as his old man; Keller, the French-hating ex-Bundeswehr Panzer driver, was looking for adventure and the chance to outdo his father's experience in the Wehrmacht; and the Turk, an Istanbul pickpocket, could put anything in his stomach and always found humor in the depths of depression. These eight were seldom separated during their years of service.

Every morning before roll call, they would assemble in the exercise yard. With hands thrust deep into overcoat pockets and collars turned up against the bitter wind, they would vigorously pace back and forth from one end of the compound to the next, hearing only the crunch of white gravel beneath their feet. Occasionally someone would talk nervously about the latest rumor spread by the last group to visit the security interrogator, but mostly they remained lost in their own thoughts until the spell was broken by the duty NCO's whistle to fall in.

Exaggerated tales of grueling interrogations made the rounds of the EVs, a group which now had swollen to about a hundred with new arrivals. The Security Bureau seeks to find out who one is, where he came from, and why he wants to join the Legion. This information is usually easy enough to obtain if a person has a passport. The real name and where he comes from can be easily discovered; only why he wants to join the Legion is left in doubt. Once the interrogator believes the man, his "envelope of secrets" is safely filed away, he is given an identity card with his alias, and he is sent on his way to Corsica for training.

The problem arises when persons with no valid form of identification seek to enlist in the Legion. Then the interrogator must question them until he believes their story. A person joining the Legion in this manner is highly suspect, and extra means of determining his identity are used, such as consulting Interpol or the *Bundes List* (a list of wanted criminals sent by the German police to the Legion Security Bureau every month).

Major criminals are rarely admitted to the Legion. The price on their heads is too high and the risk of letting a known assassin into the Legion is too great. Once these undesirable types are rooted out, they are usually turned over or traded to the French police for desired favors. The French police in turn trade them to the police of their country of origin.

Every effort is made to extract the truth from unidentified volunteers. Methods range from ceaseless interrogations to solitary confinement. If the Security Bureau cannot discover a man's true identity and they believe he is trying to join the Legion in order to elude the hangman, he is usually rejected as "unfit for service for security reasons." Murder, rape, and other major crimes would fall into this category.

Minor crimes are disregarded; most Legionnaires are guilty of some small crime or another. Desertion of family is probably the most common. Many wives call the Security Bureau in Aubagne seeking information on their wayward husbands.

Brooks's own experience with the Security Bureau was as follows:

Adjutant (interrogator) (with heavy Scandinavian accent): Come in and sit down.

A light shone in Brooks's eyes. He could see nothing. It reminded him of an old James Cagney movie.

Interrogator: What is your *real* name?

Brooks: William Brooks.

Interrogator: What is your Legion name?

B: Walter Bride.

Interrogator: What is your *real* name?

B: William Brooks.

Interrogator: Where is your passport?

B: You have it, I presume.

Interrogator: Where is your *other* passport?

B: I don't have another passport!

Interrogator: But you know how to get one, don't you?

B: No.

Interrogator: What is your *real* name?

B: William Brooks.

Interrogator: Where is your English passport?

B: I don't have an English passport.

Interrogator: But you know how to get one, don't you?

And so it went for two hours, after which Brooks was handed a five-page document in French.

"Do you wish to join the Legion after everything you have seen for the past three weeks?" the interrogator asked.

"Yes," Brooks replied.

"Then sign here."

"Walter Bride?"

"No," he said. "Sign your real name. Walter Bride isn't your real name. If you signed Walter Bride, it wouldn't be valid."

Brooks signed the paper without the slightest idea of what was on it, handed back the pen the interrogator had given him, and left the room: he was Legionnaire Walter Bride, the name he used for the next three years and eight months.

The others in his group were accepted as well, and all awaited transport to Corsica to resume basic training. They had their new clothing issue.

On Friday evening of the third week, the men boarded a ferry in the harbor of Marseille and set off for Calvi, the citadel township located on the western coast of Corsica and headquarters of the 2nd Legion Parachute Regiment.

Aboard ship the men were assigned sixth-class compartments in the hold. Everyone was given a lawn chair and made to sit elbow to elbow, while about three hundred Arabs, complete with livestock, moved in, too. After about two hours of rough seas, everyone became seasick, and vomiting became widespread. Soon the toilets were blocked. Throughout the whole sleepless night, women wailed and babies cried, seasick Legionnaires threw up on one another and fights broke out, and people urinated in the corners.

The next morning, weak and tired, the men staggered off the ship at Calvi and boarded trucks for Bonifacio, a small tourist village on Corsica's southern tip.

Ten hours later, they arrived in Bonifacio. They were shown to their rooms by a Belgian lance corporal and told to sleep. The next day was Sunday, and the new Legionnaires were told they would have plenty of time for arranging their gear. Brooks chose a bunk above Peters, and after making his bed with heavy French sheets, he crawled in and fell asleep.

Sunday arrived bright and cold. Since the French military has no quartermaster laundry service, a soldier is obliged to wash his own clothes, in cold water. Time for this is always alloted on Sunday morning. If one has the misfortune to have duty on Sunday, he must then go for another week wearing the same dirty clothes.

Because the Legion issued only two sets of fatigues and four changes of underwear per man, remaining clean became a major concern of everyone—Frenchmen excluded. During Brooks's career with the Legion he found these Frenchmen to be totally lacking in even the most basic forms of hygiene. The filthy conditions in the barracks, mess halls, and latrines were completely acceptable to his French comrades. The other groups, especially the Germans, seemed to deplore it but dismiss it all as "typically French."

A Frenchman told Brooks that it was not feasible to clean the latrines. "Why clean the latrines?" he said. "Latrines are where you shit—shit is dirty, so the shit house is dirty."

The men were allowed to shower only twice a week for five minutes. They changed their sheets twice in four months, and they accepted dogs and cats as eating companions in the mess hall. The old U.S. Army "G.I. Party" was unheard-of in the Legion. Brooks never once saw a Legionnaire on all fours scrubbing anything—it simply was not required. Dry cleaning didn't exist; wool uniforms were merely brushed and ironed by hand. Spit-shining boots and polishing brass were also nonexistent. The French never heard of such things.

Brooks on one occasion went to formation wearing a T-shirt beneath his fatigue jacket. An NCO approached, looked at the T-shirt showing under Brooks's neck, and asked him if he was cold. When Brooks didn't understand what the NCO was talking about, the NCO explained that one only wore an undershirt if one were cold. Brooks tried to explain that an undershirt absorbs body perspiration, and since he had only two fatigue shirts, it was necessary to keep a clean garment next to his

Corporal Walter Bride (William Brooks's Legion *nom de guerre*), carrying a French light machine gun at Camp Gabode, Djibouti, June, 1975. (Private collection of William Brooks.)

skin. The NCO looked dumbfounded, shrugged his shoulders, and walked away mumbling about "rich Americans."

The total lack of hygiene became acutely apparent after about ten days. The slightest cut on one's face or hand swelled overnight into a festering wound. Blood poisoning and hideous skin sores abounded. The medical personnel at the infirmary were unable to offer any treatment or prevention. Penicillin was forbidden because it "cost too much." As a result, many recruits were made to endure Legion training while suffering from scores of ugly open infections that marked their faces and hands.

Brooks asked his platoon leader, a man whom he respected, why measures were not taken to clean up the camp and provide proper medical treatment for the many poor devils caught up in this sickening situation.

This man looked at Brooks and responded: "We are not like the American Army. We have neither the time, nor the money. France is poor, you must make do as best you can."

"And how about the sheets?" Brooks asked. "They are turning black from dirt."

"To wash the sheets takes too much water. Run along now, you'll get along: Americans always improvise." The Legion placed emphasis on blind obedience. Orders were to be obeyed, without a second thought, and punishment was handed out swiftly to slackers and gold-bricks. *Schlappmacher* (goldbricker), *clodo* (bum), *penner* (vagrant), and *salaud* (filth) were words that widened Brooks's vocabulary and which were usually followed by a sergeant's slap to the face or a kick in the shin.

The French Foreign Legion was a world where orders were never questioned. Hard labor was handed out for minor offenses against regulations, together with confinement to a bedless cell block for a certain number of nights, usually from three to forty-five, combined with a twelve-hour workday digging ditches or moving boulders. Moving boulders was a favorite pastime on Corsica.

Major offenders were subjected to the *pelote*, an exercise which consisted of alternately running and duck-walking around a circle with a pack full of rocks on one's back. The maximum time alloted was twelve minutes. Brooks witnessed one Legionnaire doing the *pelote* who lasted eight minutes before passing out. He was then dragged to his feet by his ears and kicked back to his cell.

The most serious offenders were sent to the Legion's "Reeducation Camp," a penal institution located two kilometers from Corte and officially known as Le Domaine Saint-Jean. There may be no tougher military prison in the Western world. If a Legionnaire successfully passes six months there, he is usually given another alias and sent to a different unit. If he is considered to be nonreeducable, he may be thrown out of the Legion.

As well as emphasis on obedience, importance was also placed on physical conditioning. Forced marches were commonplace, and no one went through Legion training without soaking his socks more than once with his own blood. Marksmanship was also emphasized. Only the prone position was used, during both day and night firing exercises. Failure to score well on the rifle range was penalized by making the man somersault the two hundred or three hundred meters back to the firing line. Scores were checked at the targets, which resulted in the entire firing line running back and forth from the shooting stand to the target after every five-round volley.

There was no bayonet training nor were there any night maneuvers. At night, in the dark, someone may sneak off: the Legion was always afraid men were going to desert. That is why they were never paid. During the year Brooks was on Corsica his money went to a bank and he was given an allotment of $30 or $40 a month. If you had no money, you couldn't buy a ticket off the island.

The condition of the weapons was deplorable. Rifle barrels were pitted and cleaning techniques were crude. Bore cleaner was nonexistent, as was rifle oil. Weapons were oiled with 10W30 motor oil and in some cases with crankcase oil. Live firing practice was conducted two days a week for thirteen weeks.

Time was also spent on the manual of arms and close order drill. In this field, the French showed a complete lack of imagination. The manual of arms consisted of only five commands: Attention, Right Shoulder Arms, Order Arms, Present Arms, and Rest. Marching commands consisted of Forward March, Right/Left Turn. and Halt. That was all.

A soldier of fortune on sentry duty in Rhodesia. *(Private collection of William Brooks.)*

William Brooks (Chapters 5 and 6) standing guard on the railway linking Addis Ababa, Ethiopia, with the Gulf of Aden. Brooks had served with the U.S. 82nd Airborne and also saw action in the Dominican Republic and Vietnam. *(Private collection of William Brooks.)*

Legionnaires from Brooks's unit engage in target practice in the Djibouti desert. Life was hard, pay was low, wine and flesh were cheap. *(Private collection of William Brooks.)*

Michael Echanis (Chapter 10), one of the most lethal practitioners of martial arts, demonstrates a method of dispatching the enemy with a knife. Lightning speed and deadly violence were integral in Echanis's style of hand-to-hand combat. *(Private collection of Robert K. Brown.)*

(RIGHT) Heavy cattle rustling by terrorists who kill men as well as cattle forced ranchers in Rhodesia to hire mercs as security guards. The American merc here, a Vietnam veteran, is armed with an Uzi 9mm submachine gun and a .45 caliber automatic. *(Private collection of Robert K. Brown.)*

(LEFT) Echanis was as skilled in killing with his bare hands as with a knife or other device. He was considered by his contemporaries to be the most deadly martial artist alive. *(Private collection of Robert K. Brown.)*

Captain John Early (Chapter 11) in his Rhodesian dress uniform. Early, who fought for four years in Vietnam, served one year as a Rhodesian parachute instructor and two years with the elite Selous Scouts. *(Private collection of John Early.)*

Heavily armored German manufactured Unimog truck, filled with Selous Scouts, returns from a raid into Mozambique. *(Private collection of John Early.)*

The Selous Scouts, disguised and displaying the Frelimo flag, as they appeared returning from the cross-border raid described in Chapter 11. *(Private collection of John Early.)*

e "Black Devils"
nored unit, led by
ajor Darrell Winkler
Ohio, burns huts
merly occupied
Rhodesian "terrs."
*ourtesy of John
awford.)

Former Florida policeman Jack Wilkie, now a captain in the Rhodesian Guard Force, inspects his troops. The Guard Force provides protection for threatened ranches and farms. (*Private collection of Robert K. Brown.*)

Serving as security guards on a large ranch in Rhodesia: (left to right) author Robert K. Brown, armed with a Model 870 Remington shotgun; George Mullen with a Heckler and Kock 91 assault rifle; James Knapp and Scott Caldwell, both carrying FN assault rifles. The vehicle is an armored and mine-proofed Land Rover. (*Private collection of Robert K. Brown.*)

Soldiers on a 4 × 4 truck armed with a .50 caliber machine gun burn a terrorist hut. (*Courtesy of John Crawford.*)

Precision was nonexistent. Close order drill in the Foreign Legion was pathetic. Many times while Brooks paraded with the Legion he thought of the sweat he had shed on the drill field ten years previously as a military school cadet, and how the cadets had been instructed to snap heads to the right on passing the reviewing stand. They had never needed to hear the order, only watch the guidon and count. In the Legion it was a major accomplishment just to keep everyone in step.

Brooks's friend Brunin, who had served in the Irish Guards, once remarked, "How do you expect these bloody frogs to do an Eyes Right? They can't even bathe."

What the Legion lacked in sophisticated close order drill, however, it made up for by singing. Legionnaires sing everywhere they go. In fact, singing in the Legion is *canonical*. If you march into camp from the day's training and sing poorly, you must practice all night.

Hours of free time are spent marching in place by one's bunk, songbook in hand, singing at the top of one's lungs in French or in German. Most of the time one never knew what the words meant, but singing lifted spirits and lightened the load.

In the Legion, only basic instruction was administered to everyone. Whether one mastered what he was taught on Corsica was irrelevant. He could always be used as a floor sweeper. Advanced training was given only to those deemed fit by the company commander. This entailed attending an eight-week Corporal's Course, considered to be one of the most physically demanding schools the Legion runs. If one passed this course, he might be admitted to a fourteen-week NCO course, after which he would receive a chief corporal's rating and be placed on probation, awaiting orders to receive his NCO stripes. To receive the rank of NCO (sergeant) in the course of one's first five-year enlistment is exceptional. Many men spend fifteen years in the Legion and never rise above the grade of Legionnaire. This is not usually characteristic of other Western armies.

The rank system of the Legion creates a strict dividing line between grades. Legionnaires and corporals eat and sleep in the same facilities. Chief corporals eat and sleep in the same facilities as do the lower grades but have separate areas, segregating them from the others. NCOs live and eat in a separate building, as do the officers. This French concept of segregation does little to instill confidence among the troops, especially in the relationships among NCOs, enlisted personnel, and officers. The officer corps is so far removed from the Legionnaire that it made Brooks wonder just how many Legion officers had been shot in the back by their own men.

Foreign Legion officers are French, and certainly a cut above the regular French officer corps, but the troops don't know or trust them. During Brooks's tour in the Legion he met only four foreign officers, all in the junior grade. A foreigner in the Legion officer corps will never pass the rank of captain even if he remains in the Legion thirty years.

Once the training period in Bonifacio had ended, the Legionnaires marched one hundred kilometers north to the town of Corte, arriving in late May, 1972. Most of them were then sent to a specialty school operating in one of the three Legion posts located in or near this mountain town.

Brooks was assigned to a twelve-week communications course, called "Stage Transmission." The course had about forty trainees, some with as much as two years' service. Again they were forced to live in cramped quarters with barely enough space to walk between the double bunks. The weather had turned hot, the temperature began to climb, and flies swarmed over everything. The French had not heard of window screens.

Here the men were allowed showers five times a week and were given ample time to study. As the course was taught in French, studying was mandatory for anyone not knowing the language. The French students had no problems and usually sneaked out of the study room in order to drink beer at a bordello.

If one army in the world could claim holding a monopoly on alcoholics, it is the Legion. Misuse of alcohol is rampant throughout, and although it is officially discouraged, it is simultaneously encouraged. Holidays such as Christmas, New Year's, Kings' Festivals, Camerone, and Bastille Day (July 14) are all celebrated by providing large amounts of beer and wine to people who can't handle it. Beer and wine are also issued at mealtime and considered a must for the morning 9:00 A.M. snack. When one shows up drunk for duty, however, he is thrown in jail for thirty days. While in jail he is still issued his wine ration, and once he is released he merely resumes his old habits. Beer is hidden in wall lockers, under beds, and in desk drawers. It is drunk cold, warm, or hot at any time of the day. It's not a drink; it's a drug. An enemy can always trace the Legion simply by following the trail of broken beer bottles.

After the eighth week of Stage Transmission, Brooks was convinced he would never make a good communications operator. He had no ear for the Morse Code and could not pass 480 letters per minute. Besides, he had now been in the Legion for almost a year.

Brooks asked the commandant if he could be transferred to the Republic of Djibouti, then officially known as the French Territory of the Afars and Issas, but commonly referred to as just Djibouti. The application was approved and on January 9, 1973, Brooks left the island of Corsica and returned to the transit company of the Legion at Aubagne. These orders were cut for Djibouti and Brooks was issued hot weather gear and given shots and an ill-fitting wool civilian suit. He was told to wear civilian clothes on the trip over, in case the plane was forced down in Egypt or some other country where the French would not want to admit transporting troops.

On February 13, 1973, Brooks arrived at Djibouti Airport and was quickly transported to Camp Gabode, about two kilometers away, situated on the outskirts of the city of Djibouti itself. Camp Gabode was occupied by the Command Support and Services Company and the 2nd Work Company of the 13th Demi-Brigade of the Legion. Their function was to provide all the needs for the exterior companies. The "Exteriors," as they were called, were the peacekeeping forces located in border forts along the frontiers of Somalia and Ethiopia.

The 13th DBLE numbered about twelve hundred men, each of four "exterior companies" containing about one hundred fifty men, plus the four hundred or so personnel stationed at Gabode. The Legion here was still in the nineteenth century. Troops slept in old, plank-floored, wooden barracks cooled by ceiling fans and surrounded by fifteen-foot-high hedges. The hedges kept out the heat and also the dust.

Clad in kepi, neck scarf, camouflage jacket, and khaki hot pants, Brooks felt he cut quite a figure. He spent his time at Gabode getting used to his new environment. This, at last, was the *real* Legion: "Africa, continent of adventure, I have arrived at last."

CHAPTER 6

Brooks in the Legion: Africa and Action

At Gabode, Brooks met Brunin, who had been there for a number of months and who was assigned to the HQ Protection Unit of the Command Company. Brunin also worked in a general repair shop and lived with his section in a wooden barracks on the backward fringes of the camp.

Upon arrival, Brooks noticed many homemade cages and bird traps littering the sand around the barracks. Each cage seemed to be occupied by a large number of chirping field sparrows, large land turtles, and a few cats.

"What do you do with these, Brunin?" Brooks asked.

"Oh, we eat 'em," he said seriously. "You never get enough to eat around here, and if you go to a *compagnie exterieur* you'll be on the bloody frontier with nothing at all to eat but that damn Portuguese beefsteak [Legion jargon for a can of sardines]. You better hope you get assigned here to Gabode. It's better, you know."

Brooks entered the doorway of Brunin's barracks through a mosquito net and sat down on his neatly made bunk, which was covered by a colorful Arab blanket, as were the other bunks in the room.

"Don't you have to use regulation blankets?" asked Brooks.

"No," Brunin replied. "Here you do what you damn well please, no one buggers you, you know—just do like they say and you won't get beat. If you go to the frontier—"

He was interrupted by a skinny Legionnaire with a huge brown beard, black teeth, and skin the color of leather, who stuck his head through the open window and asked if Brooks was "another Johnnie." When Brunin replied, "Yes," the man asked if they wanted some cat because he was "cooking some up."

Brooks said, "Who is that?"

"Oh, that's Le Fou, he's crazy as hell, been here for eleven years. Can't go back to France, killed somebody, I think."

"What's he talkin' about, cats and all," Brooks asked.

"Oh, he's skinnin' cats this evening. Eats 'em all the time. Go look if you want."

Brooks walked to the window and looked out. Le Fou had a cat lying spread-eagled on top of an oil drum and was totally engrossed in skinning it.

"This ain't like home here," Brunin said with a grin. "Some of these people ain't nothin' but animals. You'll see, the desert is the Legion, and in the desert you live like a bloody Wog. That's how you fight 'em, by livin' just like 'em, only usin' your brain. Wogs got n' brains. Come on, Breed [Although Brooks's alias was Bride, Brunin always gave it the French pronunciation]. Let's go downtown. If you're shipped out to the frontier tomorrow, you won't get back here for maybe five or six months. Let's go to town; I'll get you a uniform and we can change your French francs for *nigger geld* [Legion jargon for Djibouti francs]. Might as well spend it. There ain't nothin' in the fuckin' *bled* [French jargon for desert] you're gonna buy."

The two men spent the hot evening drinking cold beers on the veranda of the Bar Menalik, then strolled through the human deluge of Djibouti's Quartier Deux, the main attributes of which were an overabundance of prostitutes, grossly deformed freaks, and thieves.

"Don't be afraid of these bastards," Brunin said. "They won't bother a white kepi as long as there's two. Stinkin' scum, they'll cut your throat for a fag or two."

They entered a brightly lighted shack called the "Zanzibar," pushed through a throng of outstretched hands, whores, and whiteclad local militiamen, through a second door and into a room where they stood at a bar near the juke box.

"Always stand where you can see the whores. They'll rob you blind," Brunin advised. "It ain't so bad now, 'cause none of the exterior companies are in town on *permission.* When they come in, it's the devil to pay. Trapped out there for months. You'll see. Go ahead and get drunk if you want. If you get assigned to the frontier you'll do nothin' tomorrow nohow. Liaison only come in once every three or four days. Me? I only goes to the *bled* when the colonel does; maybe I'll kill me a Wog here in town, bloody scum.

"They almost had a riot when [President Georges] Pompidou came for a visit last January. Posted me on the bridge with my rifle loaded. If we had a riot, I didn't want no *fusil,* no sir, give me an axe handle any day. It ain't like home, Breed. You'll see. If you're on the frontier least you can kill you a Wog. Here we just feed 'em. Bloody scum, look at 'em. All them nigger lovers in England oughta come over here.

"Can't even get a taxi in London no more, not even a Queen's Guard in uniform, everything polluted by the bloody Wogs. Come on, Breed, let's drink up! Ever notice how a Wog smells? You smell 'em, you'll smell 'em in the middle of the night when you're layin' in the rocks at Guister or Doumeira, when they're comin' to slit your throat. You'll see, Breed, you'll see and you'll probably love it."

The more Brunin drank, the more he talked. Brunin was Brooks's reception committee: he told him all he wanted to hear. He'd been there eight months. He was a *Vieux* (old timer): Brooks was the *Bleu* (tenderfoot). Brunin went on:

"You can desert from the frontier if you want. Go right on over to the Wogs, go to Ethiopia, though, not Somali. Too many Russians in Somali. If the Somali get you, they'll throw you so far back in a dungeon they'll have to feed you with a slingshot. Beat you around and send you back. But Ethiopians will send you to the consulate in Addis Ababa. Being an American you'd have it made. Frogs are all sent back here if they're caught. Two Germans went last fall, made it too. The adjutant got a letter from one. They let the foreigners go, only send back the Frogs."

"Trying to keep good relations maybe," Brooks commented.

"Who knows," he continued. "Who cares, bloody Frogs any way. Bad as the fuckin' Wogs. Don't know how many people desert from the frontier. Never see 'em. If they're caught they're kept at the company, and that's bad. Make 'em do the *pelote* in the exterior companies. Can't do it at Gabode, too much rank around. *Gendarmes*, naval officers, they all eat at the mess at Gabode, bad for the Legion seein' a poor bugger doing the *pelote*. You'll see, Breed, this is the real Legion, not them blokes ass-sittin' in Corte. I just hope I can shoot me a Wog."

"Let's go," Brooks said. "I've seen enough."

"Yeah," Brunin replied. "You reckon you'll go to the frontier? Bad place it is, but fun I reckon."

"I don't know, Brunin. I'll see in the morning."

Morning arrived hot as ever. Brooks reported to the placement office and was assigned to the 4th Company stationed at Holl-Holl. The liaison arrived that afternoon. Brooks said goodby to Brunin, boarded the truck along with four others, and positioned himself as best he could to absorb the shocks of the forty-kilometer ride across rocky desert.

The Legionnaires arrived at Holl-Holl, and Brooks was assigned to the 3rd Platoon as a light machine gunner. Since there was no one in the platoon's barracks who could speak English, Brooks conversed with his German *camarade* Keller. The barracks at Holl-Holl were more spacious than at Gabode, and in the desert one had a chance to really breathe. Four nights a week movies were shown, and prostitutes were provided for the Legion in the government-sponsored bordello, the BMC (Bordello Militaire Controllée). Six whores and one hundred thirty Legionnaires, however, was not Brooks's idea of romance.

"What do you want?" said Keller. "If every Legionnaire had a whore there would be a hundred whores, then the damn *schwein* would come across the wire and cut our throats while we slept. *So fast alles Arabe ... Drecke hunde.*

The only other English-speaking person in the post was an Englishman named Schutt, and he and Brooks struck up a friendly relationship. Schutt had two years' service and was well acquainted with Brunin, whom he called Patty.

"All Irishmen are Patties," he said. "Just like all Englishspeaking persons here are Johnnies."

"And just like all Wogs live south of Calais," Brooks responded.

"Oh, you've talked with Patty, all right," Schutt said laughingly. "But once you've seen these Frogs in action you'll know why we say at home, 'Wogs begin at Calais.'"

[Calais is the entrance port to France opposite Great Britain.]

"I know already," Brooks said. "It's easy enough to see how they've lost every war they've fought for the last hundred years."

"You're too serious, Billy," Schutt said. "Take the French for what they are, a bunch of Frogs; hang out with the Germans or the Francos [Spanish fascists]. They won't let you down. The French Foreign Legion is only as good as its worst German Legionnaire."

"That's true," Brooks said. And the longer he stayed, the truer it became.

The post at Holl-Holl was officially designated Poste Lieutenant Colonel De Sairigne, named for an officer of the 13th DBLE killed in Indochina. The post was situated on the Djibouti-Addis-Ababa Railroad at the point where it crossed a bridge over a riverbed. The riverbed was dry 360 days a year, but it turned into a rapidly moving torrent when it rained. The mission of the company was to protect the bridge.

Two men guarded the bridge day and night, one posted at either end. Two sandbag bunkers were also strategically placed and protected by a light machine gun kept in the guardhouse except at night, when it was placed in battery. The bridge was surrounded by barbed wire that usually washed away after rainfall and had to be replaced.

If "suspicious persons" were thought to be in the area, a threeman guard was established underneath the bridge. The Djibouti-Addis-Ababa "Express" crept over the bridge four times daily, carrying commercial and military supplies destined for the Ethiopian government. Djibouti was the only major Ethiopian outlet to the sea. The port link of Massawa-Asmara was occupied by Eritrean rebels, who had become more and more audacious after the death of Emperor Haile Selassie and the beginning of Ethiopia's drift toward Marxism.

The 4th Company was divided into five platoons of twenty-five men each, with the exception of the Command and Service Platoon, which was somewhat larger. The other four platoons were motorized infantry. Each platoon took its turn guarding the bridge and the post and performing fatigue duties, while the other three patrolled the frontier either on foot or in trucks. This was called "touring the bush" and usually consisted of a ten-day excursion to one of the numerous frontier waterholes, setting up a defensive position and patrolling the area or reconning across the border into Ethiopia or Somalia. The majority of such time was spent digging emplacements and dreaming of something cold to drink. In the hot climate food became secondary and everyone's weight dropped considerably.

The company's third function was to guard La Barrage at Djibouti, a ten-foot-high wire fence that surrounded the landward side of the town. The fence was topped with concertina and set behind a four-foot-high double apron barbed wire emplacement about ten meters in depth. This wire was set behind a mine field ten meters deep, strewn with Stolperdraht attached to antipersonnel mines and 44mm parachute flares. The mine field lay behind another string of double-apron barbed wire three meters deep and then a double strand of concertina. Signs facing outward were painted with death's heads and marked in French and Arabic, "Mines—Danger de Mort." At every five hundred meters there was a wooden guard tower equipped with a telephone and a searchlight.

Foot patrols, roving patrols, and ambushes lay in wait for anyone who crossed La Barrage, except at Poste 6, which was controlled by French Garde Mobils. Poste 6 covered the only paved road artery into the city of Djibouti, the route Italien Djibouti-Yoboki. All persons entering the city were required to possess a valid residency card or a visitation pass approved by the French. These precautions were aimed at preventing communist insurgents from entering the city, stocking arms, and causing strikes and riots.

Brooks performed more than one hundred fifty days of duty on La Barrage, each time as corporal of the relief, changing the guards, establishing ambushes, or doing dawn foot patrols to see where *Bounjouls* (French slang for Arabs) had sneaked through the wire during the night. It never ceased to amaze Brooks how many people successfully negotiated the mines and obstacles, eluded the patrols and ambushes, and successfully entered the city undetected. No matter how much wire was strung, every night someone got through successfully.

Many, however, were not so lucky. Each tour at La Barrage was marked by death in some form, usually by people striking Stolperdraht and sending 40mm parachute flares through their torsos. When these deaths occurred on Brooks's patrol route, he had the task of extracting the fly-covered corpses from the barbed wire apron, a job he found quite distasteful. It ruined his appetite for any type of burnt meat, and for days afterwards he would wash his hands with cologne.

Service on La Barrage also entailed water ambushes. At night many insurgents would attempt to swim around the Barrage, and the Legionnaires would hide in wait in the reeds near the coast or in the bottom of a rubber raft.

Service on La Barrage, however, was totally one-sided. No person attempting to enter Djibouti illegally ever shot back. Most of the would-be infiltrators were captured at night after trapping themselves in a mine field, being caught in a blinding searchlight and scared witless by having the ground to their front and rear riddled with bullets. They were mostly half-naked illiterate scarecrows, shivering in fear before these stalwarts of imperialism festooned with weapons. If they had firearms they must have buried them before attempting their entry. What Brooks captured at La Barrage was only half-starved human misery.

Camels were a big problem. Wandering into the mine fields at night, they would set off a series of flares and mines that lit up the countryside and sent alert units scurrying to the area, only to find these big hulks standing terrified in the spotlight, their feet entangled in concertina wire. Escorting these beasts out was difficult. After years of being raised by Arabs, they inherently hated Europeans—it must be the difference in body odor. With the ability to spit, bite, and kick, a camel is a dangerous brute. Brooks never met one that wasn't as mean as a wet hornet. In fact, coaxing camels out of a mine field was just as unpleasant as extracting corpses from the wire and much more dangerous. Brooks felt that the romantic conception of sun-bronzed Legionnaires racing across the Sahara on camelback must truly have been complete fantasy: the Ships of the Desert he met were no friend of the white man.

Despite the seemingly active life Brooks was leading, he, like his comrades, was continually burdened by a feeling of loneliness. This became especially acute after his first year in Africa. He now had two years' service in the Legion and at least eighteen more months to do in Djibouti. He was now a sunburnt *Vieux*—an old-timer, a desert Legionnaire. Rare visits to the city of Djibouti on weekend permission were the only escape from the feeling of solitude. On these weekends, the *Exterieurs* were readily distinguishable from the bureaucrats and functionaries of Gabode. Scrapes and scars on elbows, hands, and knees contrasted with immaculate short khaki uniforms. The *Exterieurs* were also marked by overtanned skin, sun-splotched faces, peeling noses, and chapped lips framed by scrubbed white kepis with the bills bent upwards, cocked askew on the head or tilted lower than regulation over the eyes.

Exterieurs were the nemesis of Djibouti, making Saturday night in Dodge City look like a White House tea reception. The *Exterieurs*, their pockets stuffed with three or four months' pay, flooded the bars, restaurants, and jewelry shops. Beginning the evening with lobster, pepper steak, and beer, they would move on in groups either to the more respectable bars on the Place Menalik or to the Arab quarter where they would travel like wolves, swaggering drunkenly down the alleys and looking for fights. Bars were wrecked, teenage whores bought, sold, beaten, and knifed, goats stolen, killed, and thrown aboard trucks, merchandise poached, and food stands pillaged. The Legion MPs alone ventured against the *Exterieurs*. The local militia was detested as much as the French gendarmes. "Only a Legionnaire can arrest a Legionnaire" was the rationale, and many a skull was cracked to prove the point.

On Saturday night in Quartier Deux the Legion declared war on everyone. Pimps, perverts, prostitutes, priests, or the police, they were all the same. *Bounjouls, Salauds,* or *Arabe Scheisse.* The Legion ruled the alleys and the bars, and for all the damage done there was never much complaint. In a country whose only commodities are Coca-Cola and prostitution, the damage was more than compensated for by the money spent. In Djibouti life was quick, flesh was fast, and booze was cheap.

In March, 1974, Brooks was sent to Corporals' School at Ali-Sabieh, located about forty kilometers south of Holl-Holl, This course, which was supposed to train one to be the leader of a machine-gun team, turned out to be an eight-week endurance test. Plagued by open infections and racked with blood-soaked diarrhea, Brooks and thirty-five other *élève* (student) corporals marched up and down every hill between Ali-Sabieh and Dikhil, led by a vain, five-foot, two-inch, twenty-year-old egomaniac who called himself a lieutenant.

Because the lack of suitable drinking water had caused so many bowel problems, the men lived on hot Ethiopian Coca-Cola, salt tablets, and paregoric. They never slept. Tactical problems gave way to busywork and all-night singing lessons. To compound things, Brooks got lice and blood poisoning. Desertions were en masse: three the third week, five the fourth, five the fifth. Two NCO instructors took the men's side and openly cursed the officer, who was called *Le Petit Pedale* (the little faggot).

One of *Le Petit Pedale's* favorite games was called *tenue de campagne* (field uniform). This exercise in endurance usually took place late at night and ran until early morning. The platoon was assembled and everyone given the order to change into another uniform, usually "walking out" or "parade dress," and report back to formation in three minutes. Once this was completed another uniform was prescribed, and so forth and so on for hours on end. The last one to finish usually ended up pulling Sunday morning guard duty.

The men usually ended the game by emptying their entire issues into two duffel bags and placing one in each hand. Then, dressed in full battle gear, the men would "run" to the top of Hill 904, where they would assemble and sing songs or bark at the moon until their throats were raw. Around three or four in the morning, they would be sent to their tents to prepare for the morning inspection.

Putting up with this immature stupidity night after night, together with their own physical misery, brought the men to the point of collapse. But they played these games as best they could, because one finished what he was assigned in the Legion or else he died trying. If one washed out, it was better to desert because if one returned to his company he got *le pelote* and thirty days' hard labor. So the Legionnaires changed uniforms, ran up and down Hill 904, dumped out their wall lockers, and barked at the moon.

In the filthy latrine, another generation of pot-bellied flies was breeding. Across the border in Somalia, Russian troops were instructing Somali soldiers in night maneuvers and the use of infrared firing devices. In Ethiopia, Marxist revolutionaries were plotting the overthrow of the Lion of Judah. In Ali-Sabieh the French Foreign Legion was barking at the moon!

Finally called on the carpet by the colonel, *Le Petit Pedale* was given sixty days' arrest, the course was terminated, and after six weeks and the loss of thirty pounds, Keller and Brooks returned to Holl-Holl, Brooks's problems complicated by a toothache and an ugly discoloration in a blood-poisoned finger.

The logical procedure would have been to get in a jeep and go to the infirmary at Gabode, but things don't work so simply in the Legion. First one had to make the rounds of post, seeking out everyone in his chain of command and giving them a report on how things went at the school. Having not yet received his corporal stripes, this meant Brooks had to present himself to everyone from the corporal *Chef de Chambre* (room chief) to the CO.

Keller and Brooks went together. Keller helped Brooks along as he stumbled trancelike around the fort, finding the desired person, snapping to attention, throwing back his head, and screaming, "Elève Corporal Bride, two years and two months' service. Platoon Cara, Company Kaye, returned successfully from Platoon CM1, *à vos ordres* [at your orders], Chef [or Mon Adjutant or whatever]."

Afterwards Keller would do the same; then, still standing erect, the two would be given a handshake and told congratulations and asked a hundred questions.

"How was it?"

"Heard you had a rough go of it."

And then invariably, "What's wrong with your finger, Bride?"

"It's turning black, sir."

"Better see the Médecin-Chef at Gabode."

"Oui, Chef, *à vos ordres*, Chef."

Then moving on to the next person, they would do a repeat.

Brooks had a fever and long red lines running from his wrist to his elbow. He went to the post medic, who put the black finger in alcohol, sliced the end with a razor, and squeezed it with all his might. Brooks rose a foot off the table.

"You stupid shit," he screamed. "Give me a pain killer and let me go to bed."

"No pain killer, Johnnie," the medic said. "But you can go to bed. Tomorrow you go to Gabode and see the *Médecin-Chef.*"

That was the best news Brooks had heard in a month. He walked back to his room and began to unpack. He opened his locker to find half his things stolen. There was a bullet hole in his radio.

"Nice of them to put it back after they used it for target practice," Brooks said to himself. *"Bande de Schwein,"* he muttered and crawled into bed and fell asleep.

The next morning Brooks was admitted to the infirmary at Gabode, his finger was cut open and drained every day for five days, his ailing tooth was filled, and his infections and diarrhea were treated. He slept twelve hours a day, ate all the flycovered food he could hold, and drank gallons of cold Vichy water. In ten days he was as good as new and returned to Holl-Holl in time for the celebration of Camerone.

The next day he was given his corporal stripes and assigned command of a machine-gun team which included himself, the gunner, assistant gunner, and grenadier-voltigieur (a rifleman equipped with a grenade launcher).

Time passed swiftly. The team did its job and did it well. Brooks's only problem was his platoon commander, Adjutant Cara. Cara was a Dr. Jekyll and Mr. Hyde. When he drank, he was Hyde and a dangerous Hyde at that. He beat everyone he could—those who deserved it and those who didn't.

One hot night during the summer of 1974 the company was awakened by a series of shrill whistle blasts and cries of "Alert!" It was the first time Brooks had heard an alarm sounded in the middle of the night. He jumped out of sleep in a fright—if the Legion got you up in the middle of the night, it was for real!

The duty sergeant rushed through the barracks, crying the alarm: *"Aux armes* [to arms]!"

Everything turned into pure pandemonium—shouting, yelling, and cursing from room to room; the whole post was in an uproar.

"Sac d'alert! Tenue eamoufter longue, beret!"

"Allez! Demerdez-vous!"

"Allez! Demerdes-toi, bordel!"

"Rassemblement en cinq minutes!"

The alert was a simple thing; the men had been through it a hundred times over, but everyone also had a specific function to perform during an alert. Brooks's task was to meet his team at the ammunition bunker and draw the basic ammo load for the entire section. Someone else was responsible for drawing the weapons.

Everyone in the barracks worked with feverish excitement despite all the screaming and yelling, and in ten minutes Brooks was standing in front of the ammunition bunker, awaiting the arrival of his crew. Keller hurried by in the dark, bent almost double under the weight of a .50 caliber heavy machine gun, loudly cursing providence in general and the Legion in particular.

Brooks had just leaned back against the sandbags when he heard the unmistakable scream of Adjutant Cara.

"Bride [he always pronounced the name correctly], where are the ammo and grenades? *Bordel de merde*, I'll have your ass."

"I'm waiting for my crew," Brooks responded. "They haven't shown up. I've already signed for the stuff; I'll start loading it myself—"

"Like hell you will. No corporal of mine is going to load ammo while his crew jacks off—" He drew back his arm to strike Brooks but wasn't quick enough.

Brooks was already sprinting full speed over the sand, heading for the barracks. He hit the front door at full gallop, almost dislocating his shoulder.

Two members of his machine-gun team were sitting at the breakfast table drinking coffee and eating their bread ration while "awaiting further orders."

Robinson, who was closest to him, was a Danish beerholic and well-known gold-brick.

"Arschloch! Stehe-auf-Du! [Asshole! Get up!]" Brooks screamed. "Cara is waiting at the ammo bunker! He's gonna beat your ass bloody. Where's Bejak gone?"

Robinson was so shaken Brooks thought he was going to vomit. "I don't know, Corporal Bride, he was *Kaffeeholer* [coffee-getter] today."

"Shut up and get your ass down to the ammo shack. *AbHouen-Lauf!* [Beat it! Run!]"

Robinson ran out the door, his face twisted in fear, knowing what Cara would do to him. Cara had done it before. Just then Bejak, a Bosnian illiterate, entered the room.

"Poste de Police nix café. Poste de Police nix café. [There's no coffee at the guard house]." Looking genuinely concerned, he repeated the information. *"Poste de Police*

nix café. " Since the section was on guard duty, Bejak had volunteered to carry a pitcher of coffee to the guards, not wanting any man to go without his fair share.

Calming himself, Brooks said, "*Ça va* [That's okay], Bejak, I'll give the coffee to the guards. OK. I'll do it myself, *ça va!* You get your ass down to the ammo bunker!"

Bejak placed the pitcher of coffee on the table and walked slowly to the door. "*Lauf* [Run]!" Brooks screamed. He ran behind Bejak, pushing him on his way. Cara fortunately had disappeared for the moment, and the always reliable Bandera, the gunner, was just placing the last case on the truck.

All climbed aboard and raced toward the assembly point where they picked up personal weapons. They were the last truck in the section to arrive. Luckily for Brooks, Cara was preoccupied and didn't have time to torment him over the slow performance.

After the company was assembled and roll called—the Legion loves to call roll; it even has bed check—the Legionnaires were told that Somalian forces had crossed the frontier border at Ghuister. By the light of lanterns, maps were spread out on truck hoods and orders were issued. The men were to establish a defensive position: the company was to defend the water hole, the access road, and the fort. Brooks's section was assigned the access road.

Marching orders were issued. The men climbed aboard the trucks and raced out the gate in a cloud of dust. The anticipation of adventure, which is an element in the Legion as inseparable as filth, hard work, and alcoholism, hung in the air. They knew where they were going, Le Capitaine had told them himself! They had ammunition, grenades, and rations for three days, eight .50 caliber machine guns, and a dozen rocket launchers. They even had a mortar. They weren't that badly off for four sections of an understrength rifle company with the fifth section still in garrison.

After two hours of back-aching bouncing, Brooks's team arrived at the access road to Ghuister. Here their driver let loose. Spinning out to the right of the convoy, the truck raced for its objective amid a torrent of beer bottles and abuses thrown at it from the vehicles it passed. Brooks's men responded in kind. Cara, standing up in the front of the truck à la Rommel, was in heaven!

Camouflaging the trucks and establishing a section command post among the camel-thorn bushes proved easy enough. Brooks then posted skirmishers and set about digging in—or redigging in, seeing this was the fourth trip to this same location.

The next three days were loathsome. The team dug emplacements in the rocks while Arabs stood idly by noting the positions, then walking across the border into Somalia. The sun burned relentlessly from the cloudless sky, long camouflage trousers gave way to khaki shorts, and berets to floppy bush hats. Water ran low and was rationed to one liter per man per day, not enough to live on in this environment. The Legionnaires supplemented it with Ethiopian Coca-Cola, delivered daily from the fort by donkey. The Coke was hot and not nearly as good a thirst quencher as water, but its sugar gave a boost and the acid did wonders for burning out the layers of mucus that formed on tongues and lips from dehydration.

The men were all in a state of continual irritation, especially Cara, who spent hours sitting sullenly under his camouflage net, speaking to no one. From noon until four the white man is a useless object. In the infernal heat the men stripped to the waist and lay in foxholes under camouflage nets, trying to conserve their strength. To make things worse, they hadn't seen one Somali soldier.

Brooks's section was made up of three ten-man *groupes*. Each *groupe* had two *equipes* (teams); one *equipe de choc* (shock team) and one *equipe de feu* (fire team). There were four NCOs, six corporals, and approximately twenty Legionnaires. As is usual in the Legion, the *Chef de Section* (platoon leader) was a senior noncom, not an officer. This was Adjutant Cara.

The command post was situated on the left side of an *oued* (dry riverbed). Brooks was about two hundred meters from the Somalia border and about eight hundred meters from the fort. The *puit d'eau* (water hole) was about one hundred meters to the right rear of the center of the *oued*. It was the daily meeting ground for nomads, even more so since the arrival of the Legionnaires. The presence of the Legion always attracted persons looking for a handout. The thought that this roving mass of black scarecrows which assembled daily within talking distance of the position might contain informants in the pay of the enemy never seemed to occur to the Legion's leaders. Or if it did, Brooks was never aware of it. The Legion security officer was much too busy reading the men's mail to track down spies.

On the eve of the sixth night, Cara called Brooks, Sergeant Minini, Brooks's *Chef de Groupe*, and Corporal Balkin, the *Chef de Equipe Choc*, into Cara's tent. Sitting on an ammo case, playing with his Randall Attack knife (ordered through Brooks), Cara related his brilliant scheme. Tonight, he said, *les bounjouls* are going to attack in force and the Legionnaires are not going to be caught sleeping. Batkin was to move his *equipe* to within fifty meters of the frontier but farther off to the left of the *oued*. He would then turn right and have the *oued* to his front. The Legion position would then be like an "L."

Brooks told Cara that the base would be shorter than the arm.

"Shut up," he screamed, and told Brooks to take his machinegun team to a hilltop about one hundred meters to the rear of Batkin's team, place the machine gun in battery, and establish a point for the grenadier. Sergeant Minini was to place himself somewhere between both teams. Cara said that when the Somalis passed the border marker, the Legionnaires would have them in an "L" ambush.

Brooks mumbled, "Original," and Cara menacingly waved his attack knife in front of Brooks's face. Not wanting to be outdone, Brooks unsheathed his own Randall Attack knife and began chipping hunks out of the ammo case which Cara used for a table.

Cara's face, already permanently stained by a Johnnie Walker flush, turned crimson. "Bride," he screamed, "You'll stay on the hill 'till hell freezes over. Get out of my sight!"

"*Qui, mon Adjutant,*" Brooks replied. He saluted and walked out of the tent over to his *groupe's* area. He threw ten cans of Coca-Cola into his musette, put on his jacket, and waited for Sergeant Minini.

Cara ordered the team to take a case of ammunition, about seven hundred fifty rounds, and the heavy-barrel gun. The extra weight would be transported by Robinson and Bejak, who were already quarreling over who was going to carry what. The team moved out over the rocks and organized their position so that they could fire from the top of the hill during the day and from the base during the night. Brooks purposely moved his men thirty meters closer to the frontier so they wouldn't be shooting into the backs of their comrades.

It was turning dark and each of the men began to look for a spot to sleep, preferably one that was tarantula- and scorpion free. A two-man guard team stayed with the machine gun while the others slept.

About two hours later Brooks was roused from his sleep by the sound of vehicles. "They're coming up the oued!"

"*Aux armes! Aux armes!*"

Within one minute the whole section was in place. Cara, carrying a big white walking stick, strode out into the middle of the *oued*. He raised the stick and thrust it into the ground.

"If they pass this point, shoot!" he commanded.

Brooks jumped into Minini's foxhole and asked, "What the hell is he doing?"

"*Le cafard; il cherche les mouches le mic!*" [He has the bug; he's crazy and looking for flies!]

A patrol of Somalian regulars in Russian trucks was creeping along the *oued* in low gear. Unlike the French, the Somalis make use of their blackout lights at night. Under a clear moon, however, it was nearly as bright as day, and Brooks could make out the Somalis' distinct camouflage design.

The lead truck came to a halt and an officer dismounted and walked toward Cara. Two other soldiers disembarked and placed themselves on either side of the truck. Cara and the Somali officer began to haggle. It was ridiculous, because neither one could understand the other. The officer turned and walked back to his truck and drove away.

Cara, still standing in the middle of the *oued*, pulled out his pistol and began walking back and forth nervously. Just then Adjutant Wilson, the 2nd Section Leader, came running up.

His section was emplaced on the opposite side of the *oued*, he said breathlessly, and the 1st Section was going to block the route leading from the well to the fort.

Headquarters in Gabode had been notified and reinforcements were on the way.

Wilson asked Cara what he was going to do. Cara said he was going to stand in the middle of the *oued*. Wilson looked at him as if he were crazy and trotted off.

Brooks moved out of Minini's hole and over to his team. His gunner was cussing in Spanish and nervously patting the feed cover. Brooks started to sit down behind a rock when the sky lit up and all hell broke loose.

Parachute flares and mines went off by the dozen, machine guns began firing, red and blue tracers crossed the sky and ricocheted off rocks. Bandera the gunner went through one hundred rounds before Brooks could stop him.

"What in the hell are you shooting at?" Brooks yelled.

"Somalis!"

"Where?" Brooks asked.

Bandera didn't answer; he just laid two more long bursts into the *oued* and reloaded.

Firing was still going on but Brooks had no idea what was happening. The main point of resistance was in the area of the 2nd Section. Someone was even throwing grenades. Cara stood in the middle of the *oued*, popping away at shadows with his pistol.

Suddenly it stopped, although parachute flares were still floating lazily to the ground, giving off their characteristic fizzings, For a few seconds, no one spoke a word—then the night was shattered by a deluge of curses and oaths. In Arabic, Somalian, Spanish, Italian, French, and German the most hideously vulgar and profanely elegant epithets were exchanged between the Somalis and the Legion. For five minutes the rocks resounded to a hundred-score imprecations that damned the desert, the Legion, the Somalis, France, Arabs, niggers, Jesus Christ, the Virgin Mary, the Lord God Jehovah, and everybody's mother.

Finally, Cara told everyone to shut up.

"Bride," he yelled, "What do you see?"

"*Rien* [Nothing], *mon Adjutant*." Brooks had to yell because they were a good one hundred meters apart. Cara was still standing in the middle of the *oued*, pistol in hand.

"Minini, you and Bride run across the frontier and see what's up. Come back in five minutes."

Minini told the radio operator to tell the 2nd Section the two men were coming through. Brooks told Bandera not to shoot anything until Brooks got back. The men walked across the border and around a bend in the *oued* and into the 2nd Section's area of responsibility.

"*Putain de merde*," muttered Minini.

A body lay amongst the rocks on the far side. Another lay a few meters away.

"Must have come back on foot. Maybe some more will show up."

"I doubt it," Brooks said. "They only make a habit of doing this every month or so. Hey, sergeant! Look here. This one's still got his weapon!" He pulled an East German MP–44 assault rifle out from between the rocks. "Maybe I can keep it," he said softly.

"That's between you and Cara. Come on, let's go. This place *se pourrir* [is rotten]." They walked back down the *oued*, bumping into a five-man patrol from 2nd Section on the way. They reported the Somalis had come back on foot in platoon strength. They were now, however, a good two kilometers inside their own borders and the Legionnaires were forbidden to pursue them.

Cara, Adjutant Wilson, and a Capitaine Kaye were standing near the frontier marker.

"Two Somalis dead two hundred meters down the *oued*, 2nd Section has a patrol out," Minini said, saluting.

"Minini, pull your *Equipe Choc* back to where you were this afternoon," Cara said. "Leave Bride on the hill."

Brooks saluted but didn't say anything. He turned to walk away when Cara noticed the MP–44 strapped to his pack.

"Oh, Bride, where are you going with that Klutzkopf? *Donne moi* [give it to be]! *Donne-moi!*"

Brooks reluctantly handed Cara the MP–44 and trudged up the hill to his emplacement. Bandera was in a state of nervous anticipation. He had already recamouflaged the area and was now linking together more belts.

"How many did I get, Corporal Bride? Come on and tell me. I know I got the lot, Bride, they were on foot, must have been ten or fifteen. You saw 'em, didn't you, Robinson?"

Robinson was lying on his back, smoking a Gauloise, his legs and feet at a ninety-degree angle to his torso. "I didn't see shit, Corporal Bride. Bandera didn't either."

"*Schwein du* Robinson!" Bandera screamed and drew back his fist.

Cara yelled from the *oued* for everyone to shut up or get eight days' *pelote*. Brooks headed for his hole.

"Come on, Corporal Bride, tell me how many I got," Bandera insisted.

Brooks stopped and turned around and said, "You killed six, Bandera, and scared the rest away. You saved the company from being overrun. You can go and see for yourself in the morning."

Bandera grinned like a mule eating briars. "Maybe they'll come back. I'm gonna stand guard all night, Corporal Bride. I'm gonna sit right here behind my piece."

"You do that, Bandera. I'm going to sleep." Brooks sleepily stumbled over rocks until he reached his hole. Not bothering to take off his gear, he lay down on his back, placing his weapon against a rock. He cupped his hands behind his head and stared at the clear desert sky.

In the near distance came a short flurry of rifle fire followed by Cara's unmerciful voice screaming orders, counter-orders, and profanities. Brooks rolled over on his side and went to sleep.

Brooks and Cara continued to exist together until one day in October, 1974, when the men were training on the obstacle course. One of the obstacles was a fifteen-foot steel ladder. After Brooks negotiated this obstacle, Cara ordered him to do it again. This time, however, he was to jump to the ground from the top instead of climbing down two or three rungs. as was the usual procedure. Brooks reluctantly did as he was told, and in so doing slipped a disc in his back when he hit the ground. The next day he was in the infirmary at Gabode.

His days as an *Exterieur* were over. Brooks was assigned a soft job in the infirmary as a dental assistant, and began living a life of comparative ease. He and Brunin shared the same room in a newly erected barracks complete with showers and toilets. The toilets, however, were locked, and when one needed to answer the call of nature, he had to walk fifty meters to a filthy latrine and use the holes provided. The common practice among the French was to piss out a window, off the veranda, or on the side of the building. The place stank of stale urine.

In December, Brooks was taken off the PT-exempt list and he tried out for the Legion cross-country team. He also represented the command company in pistol matches, finishing fifth in regimental competition. In February 1975 he was deemed fit enough to attend the Legion Noncommissioned Officers' School at Oueah, where the Legion Reconnaissance Squadron was located. This was quite an honor, since most of the candidates had had more than five years' service.

The school began the last week of February and contained thirty-six *élève sous-officiers*. The training was a far cry from that to which Brooks had previously been subjected. The lieutenant in charge was an excellent officer as were three NCO instructors. The students developed a comradeship within their group, which made them seem special. Their military bearing set a good example for others. The men received extensive training in desert navigation and nighttime commando operations. Brooks's French improved considerably.

After the fourth week the group moved to the tent city of Ali-Sabieh, where Brooks had suffered a year earlier. A shower stall had since been constructed, and daily bathing certainly helped prevent many of the infections which had plagued Brooks a year before. The water, however, was still undrinkable in its natural state.

By April, when the course had almost been completed, disaster struck. The Ethiopian government flip-flopped. Ever since the overthrow of Haile Selassie, the Ethiopians had remained basically pro-France in order to retain use of the Djibouti-Addis-Ababa Railroad, and that area had been comparatively stable. Suddenly, however, the Ethiopians launched an all-out attack against the rebels in Asmara.

In Djibouti itself a bomb went off in front of the Chamber of Deputies and riots broke out in the streets. All troops in the territory were placed on alert and two companies of Legion paratroops were flown in from Calvi (Corsica).

At school, Brooks and the other students were instructed to accelerate their learning and were also required to perform security duties, such as patrolling the rail lines from Ali-Sabieh to Daovenie. A double guard was posted around the camp.

During the first week in April Brooks had been informed that he would be leaving the territory and returning to France the last week of June. This news lifted his spirits, but he was convinced now that a major war was going to break out between Ethiopia and Somalia with the French in the middle. Brooks wanted to get to see it and began to volunteer for everything: night patrol, railroad patrol, border patrol.

Extra duties, however, didn't deter the students from the course of study. They assumed they would soon be making good use of what they were learning, and they combined their instruction and their security missions. Sometimes the whole class would form into an infantry platoon and sweep the frontier, crossing the border into Ethiopia at night.

It was a platoon leader's dream: every man only a few days from being promoted to the coveted Legion *Sous-Officier*. Commands were not necessary. The men moved like well-oiled machines, each one taking his turn as team leader, squad leader, and platoon chief. They were quick to obey and quick to question. On Sunday, April 27, 1975, they took their final test and everyone passed. The group had lost only six men during the eight weeks, due primarily to disciplinary problems.

That night the men cooked a freshly slaughtered goat and drank pinard. Some got drunk. Around midnight the lieutenant entered Brooks's tent and asked him who else wasn't drunk.

Brooks mentioned a few names and the lieutenant said: "Good, I'll go wake them up. You get dressed, get a PM [submachine gun], two full magazines, and some defensive grenades. Take your canteen and blacken your face; meet me in ten minutes outside my tent."

"*Oui, mon Lieutenant*," Brooks said sleepily.

Another ambush, he thought. Why him this time though? He was tired. What the hell, he thought, tomorrow they would be back at Gabode. Maybe they'd see some armed *bounjouls*.

Brooks waited outside the lieutenant's tent. Six men showed up. They were told to occupy the ground four kilometers from Ali-Sabieh next to Fort Daovenie. They were to watch the trail and the railroad, report anything that looked suspicious, and stop anyone who was armed.

"And stay awake!" the lieutenant concluded.

There was no tension—it looked routine. Brooks had been doing it for two and a half years. The men advanced to the base of the hill and placed themselves in position to fire upwards. Brooks was on the extreme right, about five meters from the railroad. He could see the lights in Daovenie and the road running up from Ethiopia, ending at a pigpen. He opened his canteen and began to drink; everybody else was just as relaxed. The *Belge* and the Greek were smoking and clanking the ammo belts and machine-gun bipod against the rocks.

Suddenly Brooks heard a truck engine. His throat froze. He felt like vomiting: it was an Ethiopian squad, jumping off the trail and moving down the railroad. Five, six, seven, eight, Brooks counted.

One was coming right up the tracks toward Brooks, a banana clip plainly silhouetted in his weapon. Brooks dropped his canteen and picked up his PM and screamed.

He was squeezing the trigger. The twenty-round magazine almost emptied in one long burst. Immediately, the machine gun opened up. Brooks slammed his face down on the ground and tried to reload but his second magazine had fallen among the rocks.

Suddenly everybody was shooting. Brooks looked up over a rock and fired another short burst, emptying his weapon. Then, again, he hid his face in the sand.

Then it all stopped. The truck was no longer in sight, although Brooks could hear its engine whining in low gear. Lights were on all over Daovenie and trucks were racing to the rescue from Ali-Sabieh, headlights on full beam! There was much nervous chatter when the lieutenant arrived. The men were all called in, and he made out a report which everyone signed.

By this time it was close to 4:00 A.M. The Legionnaires walked to the mess hall and had coffee. When they returned, a company of AMX 13 tanks was moving into the area.

"Let's all go over and see what happened last night," the lieutenant said. "I gotta make sure it's right."

The men threw their gear in the large T–46 truck and boarded a smaller VLR. They arrived at the area at first light.

"Come look at this, lieutenant," someone called, and they all walked down the tracks together.

Brooks passed the MG emplacement and noticed about fifty spent cases on the ground. Approaching a group of officers, the men saluted. The officers were standing over a corpse. His weapon was missing but his ammo pouches were for an AK–47. The rim of his camouflage hat had dropped around his neck. The top of his head was blown off.

"Somali or Ethiopian?" Brooks asked.

"Issas [Somali], by the build," someone replied.

"More blood by the crest, someone else was hit too," an excited young Legionnaire blurted out.

"Nice work, lieutenant," said an army colonel.

"Merci, mon Colonel."

"Nice work, Bride," the lieutenant repeated.

"It wasn't me, sir," said Brooks. "Badkin had the fifty-two." [AA52, light machine gun, model 1952].

"Badkin got the one on the crest," the lieutenant said. "This one is yours."

"Maybe," Brooks replied. "But I don't believe it."

Two weeks later Brooks stepped off the plane in Marseille. He had $1,000 in his pocket and two months' leave.

Leave in the Foreign Legion is called *permission*. A Legionnaire may accumulate ten days his first year and twenty days every year afterwards. Once a Legionnaire completes an overseas tour, he is given sixty days as a bonus. This sixty days may be taken when and where the Legionnaire wants only if he is an NCO. Other ranks are required to spend their leave time in designated Legion barracks and are required to sign in and out every morning, just like prison trustees. Upon completion of the NCO school Brooks was given the rank of chief corporal. Sixty days later he was promoted to sergeant, the first NCO grade. Also at this time his real identity was returned, and he stopped using the alias Bride.

During Brooks's sixty days' *permission* he was assigned to the Legion Rest Hotel located at Malmousque in Marseille. He spent a pleasant summer on the beach and traveled around the south of France. It was a real holiday. At the end of this period he returned to Aubagne and was assigned to the 1st Foreign Cavalry Regiment in Orange.

Brooks arrived there September 26, 1975. Because of his back injury, he was exempt from the infantry and was made an assistant secretary in Technical Services. The chief of Technical Services, a commandant, was assisted by three senior NCOs: one for munitions, one for gasoline, and one for vehicles. Three corporals were assistants to these three noncoms.

Brooks was given the job of accounting for the monthly consumption of fuel. At the end of every month he totaled the gasoline, oil, and antifreeze consumption and sent a report into regional HQ at Marseille. His immediate superior was Adjutant-Chef Steinmetz, a former Wehrmacht lieutenant who had about twenty-seven years' service in the Legion and was one of the finest men Brooks had ever met.

Because his job took only three or four days' work every month, Brooks had plenty of free time, which he used to good advantage. Because of his job status, Brooks was accepted and known by every officer on post. He used his position to try to seriously discuss the faults he had witnessed during four years with the Legion.

Brooks felt that if one could take the good points of the American Army and the good points of the Legion and combine them, the result would be a first-class military organization. He never knew if what he said fell on receptive ears. The Legion was too bound by traditions, which pleased no one. For example, the Legion's two greatest celebrations, Camerone and Christmas, are, for the Legionnaire, a pain. Preparations involve a series of endless work details, decorating, and, at Christmas cutting trees and setting up *crêches* (manger scenes) in every barracks room. These scenes are then inspected and judged by the colonel. The Legionnaires are rewarded with a bottle of pinard.

Brooks found the idea of a bunch of Legionnaires being forced to construct elaborate manger scenes a trifle hypocritical. All men were confined to post the night before Christmas, and the Christ child was saluted by a compulsory roaring drunk that began in the mess hall at midnight. Brooks was not alone in his feelings. One Christmas a *crèche* constructed by some Legionnaire humorist contained the nativity scene offset by a human skull placed near the baby Jesus.

As Brooks's five-year tour neared its end, he exaggerated his military appearance. His boots were too shiny and fatigues too well pressed. He starched his fatigues by hand—the French had never heard of starch. Brooks overexaggerated his "pot-to," slapping his side, throwing his head back, and blurting out, *"Mes respects, mon Lieutenant."*

Brooks lost himself in books on the OAS (*Organisation Armée Secrète*—Secret Army Organization) and the putsch of 1961. He read and reread stories of the anti-Gaullist Vichy *milice* and the courageous battle of the German-sponsored French SS in World War II. He convinced himself that there were good French soldiers.

Brooks drove Steinmetz crazy with questions. "Were the French as sorry twenty-five years ago? How would you compare the Wehrmacht with the Legion? Have you ever met a Frenchman who knew how to use a toilet?"

One day the NCO mess was visited by the commanding general of the Foreign Legion. Attendance, in formal attire, was mandatory. After a few minutes of introduction, the general rose to speak. "The Role of the Legion Today" was his subject, and he explained the disposition of troops by regiment and the situation in each area, particular emphasis being placed on the situation in Djibouti. The NCO corps listened intently, grimfaced and serious.

The general then said, "The Legion will always be a modern arm within a modern army."

"A modern arm within a modem army," Brooks repeated to himself. Then he started to smile. He wanted to burst out laughing. He surveyed the room. The NCOs were totally engrossed in the general's speech. There wasn't one smile among them, not even a smirk. Brooks felt as if he were adrift at sea; the general was still talking but Brooks heard nothing. He felt drunk.

"A modern arm within a modern army." He repeated the words over and over in his mind. "My God," he thought, "they actually believe it, look at them, they believe it, they really believe it!!!" Brooks was dumbfounded. When the general's speech ended, he excused himself from the table and went to his room. He lay down on his bed and placed a towel over his eyes.

"They have convinced themselves, the damn fools; they have convinced themselves, the bloody, beautiful fools!"

On January 19, 1977, Brooks left the French Foreign Legion. In his suitcase was his honorable discharge, signed by Lieutenant Colonel Tribout, an officer he had never seen or met. Brooks was neither happy nor sad. He felt that he was still a Legionnaire in spirit. He took a train to Paris.

Just short of two weeks later he boarded a plane for New York, and nine hours later he was circling John F. Kennedy Airport where the runways were slick and it was depressingly overcast. The plane circled overhead for forty minutes. Then it made its approach, the wheels touched down, and it came to a halt alongside the terminal. Brooks found his kit bag and approached the customs counter.

"What do you have in here?" a customs inspector asked, pointing to Brooks's bag.

"Personal items," Brooks replied.

"Open it and let me see," he commanded. "Are you military?"

"Yes sir," said Brooks.

The official said, "Go on through."

Brooks walked through the door, past a guard, and onto the street. It was beginning to snow.

L. H. "Mike" Williams:
Kraals and Galloping Goffles

"The guerrillas carefully dug a hole in a dirt road leading into a tribal area in Rhodesia. They gingerly placed a Russian-made TM–36 land mine in the hole. They covered the mine with earth, then realized they had to tamp down the covering soil in order to conceal the presence of the mine. Joining hands, they began jumping up and down on the mound of earth. Their heavy boots packed the soil down over the detonator, but the resulting explosion blew all three guerrillas into the top branches of a nearby baobab tree. Army patrols found their remains the following day."

Every country has its own characteristics, and each war has its distinct characteristics. No two wars are alike, as soldier of fortune L. H. "Mike" Williams, who described the above scene, found out in Rhodesia. And war in Africa certainly is unique. There was the time when Williams was leading troops in attacking a kraal where guerrillas were believed to be hiding: "In the midst of the fourth mortar round, three big crazy-ass roosters with a harem of four hens madly sauntered right through the hail of 7.62 rounds, contentedly pecking at corn husks lying on the sand." And there was the time a soldier shot a chicken belonging to a schoolmaster, and Williams had to negotiate reparations, finally making a payment of $2.50.

How does an American fighting man come to such strange doings?

Williams enlisted in the U.S. Army in 1942 and saw combat as an infantryman with the 88th Division in Italy. Choosing the military as a career, he was commissioned a second lieutenant at Fort Benning in 1948. Williams was one of the first officers assigned to the 10th Special Forces when this unit was activated in 1952. In 1953 he was ordered to Korea, where he commanded a special battalion composed of some twelve hundred Chinese and North Korean defectors. Upon returning to the States from Korea, Williams served with the Special Forces and then with the Airborne. He was discharged from the army as a captain in 1960.

In 1964, Williams joined the mercenaries led by famed Briton Michael Hoare operating out of Kamina Base in Katanga, Africa. When the United States decided it did not want Americans fighting in Katanga, Williams had to leave.

But Williams was not ready to give up fighting. He recalled the statement someone once told him, "If you spend more than ten years as a soldier, you'll never be worth a damn as anything else." In December, 1975, he headed back to Africa for the second time. His intention was to join up with the UNITA guerrillas (Chapter 8) fighting the Cuban forces in Angola. This did not work out, however, and so after a stop in Zambia, Williams traveled to Rhodesia to try to join that nation's army. The army was embroiled in a conflict with black guerrillas who continually slipped over the border from neighboring Mozambique and Zambia.

Williams made contact with the Special Branch, Rhodesia's version of the FBI, and was enlisted by that organization to do a task for it outside the country. Later, upon returning to Salisbury, the capital of Rhodesia, Williams met with an army officers' selection board. His account of the proceedings: "I gave them a detailed resume which they carefully read and obviously disbelieved. I learned later that their skepticism was based upon previous experiences, mostly unpleasant, with other Americans. They made it clear to me that there were no mercenaries in Rhodesia. The only way anyone was going to serve Rhodesia in a military capacity was as a member of the regular Rhodesian army.

"A direct commission in the grade of captain was offered me, which I accepted." (Later Williams would be promoted to the rank of major.)

Williams was first posted to the 3 Protection Company at Mount Darwin, about two hours' drive from the border with Mozambique, which was one of the guerrillas' training and staging areas. Protection companies are just that: units semi-detached from the army and assigned to protect specific areas and/or installations. Williams was informed that "officers assigned to protection companies are either too old to command firstline troops or else the army wants to keep an eye on them." Further, the troops in the companies were what was termed "unusual." The commander of 3 Company explained to Williams about his "unusual" troops: "They're colored. African mothers and European fathers, or the other way around. The Europeans shun them and the Africans hate them. They're outcasts from all levels of society."

One of 3 Company's missions was to furnish armed escorts for graders, bulldozers, and other construction equipment used in building roads. Another company responsibility was to convoy transportation to and from Mukumburu, a village near the border. To determine the combat readiness of the troops Williams rode with convoys several times. He discovered: "Generally the troops were alert but I found empty Coca-Cola bottles, tire irons, vehicle jacks, and chains thrown carelessly in the back of some trucks. This crazy practice soon ceased when I pointed out what would happen to the troops riding in the rear of the vehicles if the trucks hit mines and the Coke bottles started flying around like shrapnel."

After a month Williams was transferred to Llewellin Barracks in Bulawayo, to assume command of 5 Protection Company. This company was assigned to guard an eighty-kilometer segment of a railroad which carried petroleum, ammunition, and other vital supplies from South Africa to Rhodesia. Recognizing the importance of the rail line, guerrillas staged raids against it. These raids had become so intense that rail crews would work only during the daylight hours.

Williams put his unit through a training program and then led the men in a convoy to the area they were to guard. The rail segment ran northwest from the town of Rutenga to another called Ingezi. At Ingezi stood a bridge, the protection and maintenance of which was essential to the running of the railroad.

The problem of protecting the railroad was severe. Williams noted:

"The railway snaked and twisted through cuts whose embankments rose almost vertically on either side of the tracks. One gook with an RPG7 or even an AK with tracer, and 'goodbye, tank cars.' Further south the picture was almost as bad; open areas of five hundred to six hundred meters from which jutted kopjes or hills of rock with heavy bush providing excellent field of fire, cover and concealment.

"To complete this dismal situation, Belingwe Tribal Trust Land (TTL) on one side of the rail line was a noncurfew area with total freedom of movement for people, vehicles, and donkey carts. Directly across the tracks was Matibi 1 TTL, a curfew area and a hotbed for terrorist activities. The terrorists were no fools. They would zap the trains as they passed, then simply run across the tracks, cache their weapons, and go to the nearest beer house to celebrate.

"If the Rhodesian Army wanted to test my command capabilities, they sure as hell had picked the right situation. A company strength of two hundred to secure a bridge and eighty kilometers of rail line would have been laughable—had the situation not been as desperate as it was.

"To patrol the tracks, Rhodesia Railways had furnished us with some gasoline-powered trolleys. Small, armored vehicles, they held a civilian driver and eight troops.

"At 0200 hours on 4 June 1976, 2/Lt. Angus Scrace and five troopers were ambushed by five terrorists, who missed the trolley from a distance of about thirty meters. The terrorists evidently thought the searchlight atop the trolley was that of a locomotive and fired high. Scrace returned the fire with SLRs and a Bren gun, the trolley rattling down the track and the driver busily engaged in talking with whatever ants were crawling on the trolley floor."

Willlams decided there was absolutely no way he could adequately guard the rail line and bridge with a mere two hundred infantry soldiers. He pondered: "There would have to be a more effective means of providing troops mobility than letting them use their feet. What was more effective than two feet? Four feet, naturally. I would put my people on horses. The increase in speed and the amount of terrain they could cover in a day would be tremendous. Horses it would be."

Williams went to a local rancher and explained his idea. The rancher agreed to provide horses and tack and he put Williams in touch with other ranchers who would also cooperate. When Williams informed the area commander of his plan, the officer "apparently felt this was ample evidence that as a Texan I was not only crazy, but thought I was John Wayne as well."

Williams began training his men in combat equitation:

Major L.H. "Mike" Williams, Deputy Commander of Grey's Scouts, Rhodesia's famed mounted infantry unit. (Courtesy of *Soldier of Fortune*.)

"Horses have been implements of war since Xerxes and the Phoenicians, and I felt that given the area I had to cover, the type of terrain, and the handful of troops I had, then by God, the cavalry would ride again!

"As a second-class ride is better than a first-class walk, I had no problem getting volunteers from the colored.

"There were no formal classes in equitation. The drill was as follows: (a) bring out horse, (b) introduce 'rider' to horse and get him mounted, (c) point horse in desired direction and urge rider to stay on, (d) if required, pick up rider and take to medics.

"Strangely enough, the casualties were few. The condition of one soldier who landed head-first in a thorn bush resulted in tremendous improvement in Basic 'Equitation One' classes. People somehow managed to stay on. I set up a field expedient firing range to condition the horses to SLR fire [the SLR Williams refers to is the FN Semiautomatic rifle M1949 in 7.62mm], hand grenades, Bren guns and later Uzis. The range consisted of cardboard silhouette targets set up at ten, twenty, and thirty meters. The troopers would ride down one side, engaging the targets, do one-hundred-eighty-degree turns, and ride back, once again engaging the targets.

"Each would fire five magazines while running the course. Five hits out of a magazine was satisfactory. In fact, one hit per target by each trooper was damn good.

"Firing was done at the walk, trot, and canter, respectively.

"I also taught them to execute standard infantry formations while mounted: echelon right, echelon left, line of skirmishers, etc.

"Counter ambush drill while mounted took into account the terrain and distance from which the ambush was initiated. If the enemy opened up from fifty meters, we would use the mobility provided by the horses and try to outflank the ambush. However, most ambushes occurred between twenty-five and fifty meters. In this case we would dismount, establish a line of fire, and maneuver. Unfortunately, the horses would often bolt—which could result in a long walk back to base.

"The remainder of instruction was on-the-job training. Patrolling started along the railway. The looks from the locals were incredulous. In addition to the tremendous increase in mobility, I received an added bonus from the use of horses. The Africans were scared to death of the animals. Psychological warfare, no less."

Colored troops in the Rhodesian army are known as "goffles." Williams's strange unit became known as the "Galloping Goffles."

Williams moved his headquarters to Sarahuru, roughly midway along the rail segment. Soon after he made the move, a train was derailed by a mighty explosion that strewed cars along the line and tore up one hundred meters of track. Three nights later the line was blown again at the same place. Williams and his men went into action:

"Two guides met us about five hundred meters south of the attack site. I'd ordered the vehicles halted, debused the troops and we hiked in. The guides were with a local unit that had been fired on. They pointed out a kraal. They'd heard no dogs barking to indicate movement away from the huts.

"The Rhodesian Army discouraged field grade officers from physically leading troops, as they feel this is a subordinate's job. I had just been promoted to major and one of my subbies was in Rutenga, the other at the Ingezi Bridge.

"Forty sets of white teeth and eighty rolling eyeballs surrounded me.

"I briefed the section leaders [equivalent to U.S. Army squad leaders] with me, cautioning them about wild firing and the difficulty of control at night. We started off across a cornfield with the guides leading. Stalks of corn cracked underfoot, sounding like field artillery. I was sure we sounded like a herd of rhino. The approach march covered about three hundred meters and I could barely make out distant outlines of a large kraal. It appeared to consist of fifteen to twenty huts.

"I stopped at a fence and counted noses. All present. Past the fence and into muddy ground. My feet were sopping wet and corn stalks thudded against my SLR barrel. The five magazines in chest webbing pulled at the straps around my neck and I was sweating. The wedge formation moved into a line of skirmishers. A trail running north-south had to do as a Line of Departure (LD) [U.S. Army term for the point from which an actual assault is started]. Rhodesians call it a Start Line. LD or Start Line—when you cross it, that's when the guts start churning and the balls start retracting. I had no idea what people would do, so I took four men with me, leaving the platoon sergeant with the formation, and scouted out the nearest huts. I told him not to zap us on the way out or back. Moving out, I was aware that at this point I could get it from an AK in front or an SLR from the rear.

"Ahead of me in the kraal, nothing moved. One by one we checked the dark huts. Empty. I motioned to the patrol to head back to the waiting troops. Suddenly an AK opened up from food huts on the side of a hill, and dogs began barking like crazy from the rear of the kraal. We put up flares and commenced firing. Sighting on the dark buildings, I opened fire, sending orange tracers streaking into the food huts, and yelled an order into my Bren gunner's ear to begin 'traverse and search,' the technique of sweeping an area with short bursts of automatic fire. Tracers hit the huts, ricocheting over the ridge line to the rear of the village and turning the blackness into a fireworks display.

"Smoke, then orange flames started from the roofs of the huts and spread with the wind. By now the entire kraal was afire. We got up and assaulted, using marching fire. Two bodies and AK shell casings lay near the food huts. Charred bits of denim clung to the legs of the dead men.

"At first light choppers with Fire Force [airborne reaction force] came in, landing trackers who circled the area until they picked up spoor of eight people: tracks [of terrorists] heading from the railroad to the kraal. The trackers lost the spoor in the rocks on the ridge line. An additional three sets of tracks headed across the rail line into Belingwe TTL where the locals deliberately obliterated them by milling their cattle, whose hooves crushed all signs of terr boots.

"We counted a total of twenty-nine huts burnt, two suspects dead, and one of my people hit in the face with a piece of rock from a ricochet."

The action had occurred on a day significant to any American: July 4, 1976—the Bicentennial of the United States. For four months afterward, there were no further terrorist attacks on the railroad.

With the railroad area now quiet, Williams was transferred to Umtali to serve as temporary commander of 6 Protection Company. A primary task of 6 Company was to guard against infiltrators coming over the border from Mozambique. To help carry out this mission Williams brought in his "cavalry" from 5 Company. Although the terrain was rugged, the horses proved as useful as they had been on more level ground. Once again, the "Galloping Goffles" were a source of wonder.

When Williams led his men to an isolated artillery bivouac, "the artillery men stopped their volleyball game and watched pop-eyed as we dismounted...."

Williams led a horse reconnaissance in a mountain area in pursuit of guerrillas. The troops moved upward over a trail that narrowed as the bush became thicker. Then the men had to dismount, as the ground underfoot turned into an intermittent series of roots that could trip an animal, causing it to fall and break a leg.

The men climbed the mountain that was their objective. At first it was relatively easy to traverse, but as the troops climbed higher, the steepness and arduousness increased. Said Williams, "Our steps shortened. Breathing became more difficult. The long, easy traverses I'd originally planned on using to assault the mountain now became shorter, more difficult. Soon it became impossible to climb without using both hands."

Finally Williams reached a vantage point, and from there he could look and see, far below, five guerrillas walking in single file. They were entering a wooded area; the sun glinted off the barrel of the AK carried by one of them. But Williams could do nothing: the guerrillas had already crossed the border and were in sanctuary in Mozambique.

Williams and his men were then deployed to the Weya Tribal Trust Land, south of Salisbury. The area was plagued by guerrillas. Williams and his unit combed the Weya, searched kraals, interrogated local citizens, and tried a little of what is known in the American military as "civic action": the medic riding with the troops treated the children for coughs, eye infections, and other illnesses.

On patrol one night Williams and his troops stopped at a clearing, to take a break and water their horses. They then started up a hill. They passed a thick clump of underbrush and made a ninety-degree turn to start a long traverse across the slope.

Suddenly shots cracked from their rear. There was a burst of fire from an AK followed by a long tak-tak-tak from a light machine gun. Within five seconds a corporal riding in front of Williams was hit in the arm and Williams's horse, Bossikopf, took a grazing wound on the side of the head. Williams pushed on his right foot to steady himself but there was no stirrup. It had been shot away.

Williams jumped and landed hard. The horses bolted, scattering troops left and right. One of the troopers began returning fire, his tracers hitting the side of a ravine and ricocheting into a kraal near a wooded area.

Flashes from three more AKs indicated the presence of additional terrorists. Williams began firing. He found himself in the middle of a plowed field without any cover. He later commented: "There is no more naked feeling in the world than lying belly down in an open field bathed in bright moonlight with five terrs fifty yards away energetically trying to blow your brains out." He could see movement to his left and he snapped off several rounds in that direction.

From the sounds of dogs barking it appeared that the guerrillas were running across the field away from the troops. The machine gun ceased firing. To his right

Williams could see a clump of rocks. Several of the troopers were lying behind it, firing at the ambush point. The shooting became sporadic.

Williams yelled at a corporal behind the rocks to put up a flare. It streaked upwards, opening with a sharp pop. With the light the troops opened fire again on the ambush point. The flare would illuminate the troops as well as the guerrillas, but Williams felt that it was a chance that had to be taken: the moon was so bright that a little extra candlepower would not make much of a difference in their danger.

Drifting down and trailing sparks, the flare outlined a couple of figures running for the kraal. Tracers arced after them. One went down before he could reach a hut; the other managed to get to a heavy patch of bush at the rear of the kraal.

Williams ordered his men to get up and charge forward. They ran across the plowed field, and when they reached the huts one of the troopers threw an incendiary grenade into the first building. There was a loud thump and a fire started, flames crackling from the thatched roof. The soldiers kept moving, sweeping through the kraal. They kicked open the doors of the huts, firing whenever they thought they saw something moving.

But the occupants of the huts had fled. It had been a planned departure, not a spontaneous evacuation: the people had known there was to be an ambush and they had not wanted to stay around. A count was taken and it showed that Williams's detachment was intact. The crumpled bodies of two guerrillas were found.

The soldiers gained high ground overlooking the kraal, and for good measure Williams ordered additional fire into the kraal. The buildings were raked with automatic weapons. The entire village burned. Williams wanted "the locals [to know] our displeasure at the kind of welcome we had received."

Psychological warfare was important in this war, as it is in all conflicts. While leading a detachment in the Tjolotjo Tribal Trust Land, Williams decided to stage a firepower demonstration in an effort to deter locals from joining the guerrillas. Rocky Stone, the acting district commissioner, brought together some five hundred Africans for a meeting. Williams has described the proceedings:

"I began to speak, Rocky interpreting my words into fluent Shona.

"'I speak to the mothers among you. Raise your arms.' A sea of black hands rose. 'If you love your children, you will keep them from the lies of the terrorists.' Rocky translated furiously, sweat running down his chubby face. 'Do not let them go to Mozambique.' I glanced at one woman surrounded by children. Her eyes were wide, mouth open.

" 'We do not wish to kill your children. We want them to stay home, to go to school, to become educated.' Looks were exchanged among the crowd…. 'Ahhh!' A loud gasp of approval came from the women.

… " 'I now speak to those children among you who are thirteen years and older.'

"Self-conscious giggles and furtive looks greeted this last. 'I want you all to stand.' Slowly, goaded by their mothers' pushes, a large number of boys and a few girls stood.

" 'What you are now going to see is what will happen to you if you join the Communists and come back here as terrorists.' "

Before the crowd had arrived, Williams had placed some of his men with two machine guns on a nearby hill to the right. To the left he had set up two 60mm and two 81mm mortars. Williams now raised a hand and gave the signal to open fire.

There was pandemonium. Williams's description continues: "At the first ear-splitting cracks of the machine guns, all the youngsters standing dove into the crowd. The tracers ripping out to the target area were unseen by the vast majority of the Africans, who were howling at the tops of their lungs and burying their faces in their arms. When the mortars started firing, the unfamiliar THUMP brought several black faces up, eyes wide.

More heads were raised. Rocky seized the opportunity to give his own spiel. "The soldiers will rise as ghosts from the ground!" he yelled.

Right on cue, the sergeant in command of the assault detail gave a blast on his whistle and the riflemen, who had been lying hidden in the mealie stalks before the crowd, dramatically rose. This was too much! Half of the crowd broke and ran, streaming for the bushes at the rear of the area.

The demonstration produced an unexpected dividend: in the midst of the deafening racket of the gun and mortar fire, a woman gave birth.

As previously noted, every war has its distinct characteristics. Psychological warfare in the African bush had its unique aspects, too.

Early in July, 1977, Williams was transferred to Grey's Scouts, where he was to be second in command. Named after a Rhodesian pioneer, the Scouts, mounted troops, were one of the best-known units in the Rhodesian Army. Williams continued to serve in the bush: patrols in search of elusive guerrillas, occasional rapid fire fights, a terrorist shot while trying to evade troops, a police constable killed by a land mine. And always the African touch: three terrorists robbed a store near the town of Lupane. Getting $3.00 from the terrified storekeeper, they decided they were hungry and ordered Cokes and cookies. They then paid for these with the three dollars they had just taken.

Williams is one of the more expressive of that breed of men who are soldiers of fortune. In a book he wrote he described his feelings on one occasion when he was returning to the bush: "As usual, I had mixed emotions…. Anyone who has ever been shot at as an infantryman knows what I mean. There is an exhilaration in combat that is not evident in any other life experience. Perhaps it stems from the realization that you can survive in spite of chaos, confusion and noise. Each time you do come out it leaves you with a tremendous desire to stay away from it, but this is soon replaced with an equally intense feeling of wanting to try it again.

"Maybe some day someone will be able to put on paper a description of what the feelings are truly like. One elderly colonel came as near as anyone…. He said, 'Take two days to get worked up to it and when you come out, take two days to wind down before you talk to civilized people.' His theory worked pretty well for me."

On February 28, 1978, the Rhodesian Army and Major Mike Williams parted company. He felt that Rhodesia was fighting basically a defensive war, overly concerned about "world opinion" regarding its actions. He later wrote, "I felt like a *pistolero* who'd outlived his usefulness. There were no feelings of regret on my part; I had given them my best shot, but their methods of running a counter-insurgency war were identical to those the United States had followed in losing Viet Nam. The name of the game now was 'No Win'—there could be no military victory! No-win wars mean exactly that! No commander worth his salt is going to put up with this type of thinking for very long."

But when Williams looked through the window of the airliner which was about to take him out of Rhodesia, "It felt as if I were leaving a home behind me—not going back to one."

CHAPTER 8

George Bacon:
Fighting Against Communism

Deep in black Angola, George W. Bacon and Gary Acker, two Americans fighting under another flag, were moving slowly down a narrow dirt road that wound through the bush. It was February 14, 1976, and they were searching for a friendly patrol that had not returned. Heavily armed and dressed in sweat-stained fatigues, they combed the foliage for movement from their battered Land Rover.

Suddenly fire from AK–47s and RPD light machine guns ripped through the body of the vehicle. They had been ambushed! Bacon and Acker dove out of the Land Rover before it came to a stop. Acker took a round in the leg. Bacon, however, had come to the end of his road. His bullet-ridden body was already dying when it hit the road. With his own country now at peace, George Bacon was probably the only American killed in action fighting the communists in 1976.

George Bacon III was an environmentalist. He appreciated a clean, natural environment and he wanted a healthier political environment. So strongly did he feel about improving the world environment that he served and fought in three countries.

Special Forces medic in Vietnam, CIA case officer in Laos, recipient of the CIA's Intelligence Star, *summa cum laude* college graduate, soldier of fortune in Angola, George Washington Bacon III would be described by a friend as "a twentieth-century crusader ... a unique example of the triumph of ethics over greed, of commitment over apathy, and of action over intention." Like most intelligent, complex men, George Bacon cannot be reduced to a cardboard cutout; among other things he was a freedom fighter, dedicated anticommunist, and winner of the CIA's Intelligence Star.

Bacon was born August 4, 1946, in Biddeford, Maine and grew up in Longmeadow, Massachusetts. His compassion for people was evident even when he was a child. His younger sister wanted a tricycle and didn't have one; Bacon bought her a used one at a church bazaar. "He was always doing things like that," his mother later observed. On another occasion he was visiting his grandmother in North Carolina when he found an abandoned puppy. He adopted it and gave it to his sister as a present. Bacon loved animals, and his mother recalled that she was often apprehensive about washing his clothes for fear of finding worms or frogs in the pockets.

Bacon was fond of sports, especially swimming and deep-sea diving. A natural athlete, he was good at almost everything he tried. He was not a great athlete; but he tried hard and kept trying until the whistle blew.

One day when Bacon was in high school, the car in which he was riding caught fire, making him late for dinner with his parents. Mrs. Bacon's sister telephoned his home before Bacon arrived and told her, "I just saw George on TV in a car that was on fire!" When Bacon returned, he merely said, "Mother, I'm sorry I was late, but we had a little trouble." He was low-keyed about the incident, although his clothes reeked of smoke. According to his mother: "It was as though it didn't bother him at all. That's the way George was." This inherent ability to remain calm in hazardous situations was to prove invaluable to Bacon later in Vietnam and Laos.

After high school, Bacon attended Georgetown University, where he majored in international relations at the School of Foreign Service. It was during this time that his commitment to anticommunism and to liberating the oppressed solidified. Dr. Carroll Quigley, one of Bacon's professors, wrote what became Bacon's favorite book: *Tragedy and Hope: A History of the World in Our Time*.

In 1966, after two years at Georgetown, Bacon joined the army. It was a decision that changed the course of his life. From the abstract world of academia he plunged into the reality of the wartime army. The army suited Bacon much better than university life; it was to provide him with the opportunity to fight for what he believed.

Bacon's patriotism, though high, was tempered by the army's bungling bureaucracy. His frustration stemmed from being stuck in clerk school when Bacon wanted desperately to be in the infantry. In a letter home dated November 27, 1966, Bacon explained, "One of my good friends here at clerk school wanted to go to the infantry so badly that he purposely flunked out of here; while they assured him he would be sent to infantry, the Army sent him to cook school instead. He went AWOL and I haven't seen him since. To me, being a clerk is just one small notch above being a cook—I won't accept either one."

And in the next paragraph, "I'll desert and join the French Army, which I know takes foreign citizens into its officer corps. I'm beginning to find out that what everybody said about the Army is true—not because it is hard or challenging but because the opposite is true—at least so far."

Soon, however, Bacon was accepted into Special Forces. He became a medic after a year of arduous training and graduated at the top of his class. Bacon's fine record during his Special Forces training was a preview of his later successes in Vietnam with the Special Forces and subsequently with the CIA in Laos. Commendations piled up in his file. On December 4, 1967, he was selected as the Honor Graduate of the Special Forces medic course; on February 23, 1968, he was designated Soldier of the Month and selected as the Distinguished Honor Graduate of the Special Forces Training Group (Airborne), Class 68-5.

While in training at Fort Bragg, North Carolina, Bacon wrote his parents telling them that he was satisfied that SF was a much better choice for him than Officer Candidate School, which his father had recommended. He wrote them, "At least now I have found something at which I can become among the very best." Bacon knew that to maximize his effectiveness in Vietnam he would have to learn Vietnamese; he began studying the language with a tutor while in training, and by the time he arrived in Vietnam, he had become fluent in it. As a friend of Bacon's said, "He was an expert in Vietnamese and could speak Chinese well enough to communicate with our Nung mercenaries. I understand that when he got to Laos later he became a real authority on Meo" (it should be noted here that the dialect of the Meo mountain tribesmen with whom Bacon fought in Northern Laos is among the most difficult of all spoken languages, having never been put into any kind of printed or alphabetical form).

Bacon was not one to talk much about his combat experiences. His father recalled, "George once mentioned casually that a helicopter he was riding in was shot down. One of the troops was shot through the leg and George bandaged it for him. When the helicopter went down, it was behind enemy lines and the chopper crew panicked. George said he was able to lay down enough fire power to keep the enemy at bay until another helicopter could land and pick them up."

One of Bacon's comrades in MACV-SOG (Studies and Observation Group—the cover name used by the CIA for operations into North Vietnam, Laos, and Cambodia which were carried out by Special Forces and indigenous personnel) provided insight into Bacon's experiences in Vietnam. This man met Bacon in December, 1968 at Command & Control North (CCN) located at Da Nang. He related: "Before coming to Da Nang in August, Bacon had been running 'walkout' recons out of Khe Sanh, while the Marines would go one hundred meters outside the perimeter and get their asses blown away.

"I worked with George for three or four months in early 1969," his comrade remembered, "and he was always in the thick of things. In February, 1969, our team conducted a bomb damage assessment of what, up to that time, was the largest B–52 strike of the war—over one hundred B–52 sorties in twenty-four hours on the same target. The strike was directed against the headquarters of the North Vietnamese Army's 27th Regiment's base camp. The last bombs fell at 0730 hours and we were inserted at 0830 hours. We stayed on the ground for less than six hours. Our team consisted of eight men—three Americans and five Vietnamese.

"We were inserted in unmarked H–34 choppers manned by Vietnamese crews. Air cover was provided by four UH–1C gunships; at the time, the rules of engagement prevented tactical aircraft from operating in the area.

"We found numerous bunkers and there were NVA all around us. We had blundered into a hornet's nest. Because of the large number of enemy in the area, the powers that be considered the raid had been a success.

George Washington Bacon, left, receiving the Intelligence Star for his outstanding performance as a CIA officer in Laos from William Colby, Director of the CIA. (Courtesy of Central Intelligence Agency of U.S.A.)

"The second operation took us into the same area on a reconnaissance and prisoner snatch. We were inserted at 1100 hours. We had moved only one hundred meters away from the landing zone when we began taking heavy ground fire. Our point man took an AK round through the arm and two other Vietnamese were wounded, though they could walk.

"George and I stayed behind and held off the enemy while the team leader and remainder of the team withdrew to the LZ and established a tight perimeter on the far side. It was hot and heavy as George and I detonated Claymores, threw grenades, and fired bursts—he from his CAR–15 and myself from a silenced Swedish K. We don't know how many we got, though I heard NVA screams after I tossed a white phosphorous grenade.

"On this mission, George was the radio operator and number three in the chain of command, and I was the assistant team leader. During the fire fight, I kept telling George to get out. He would not leave. We began arguing, as we were firing, about who should stay and who could leave. In the end we compromised: both of us stayed. About fifteen minutes later, back at the perimeter of the LZ, I said, 'You ass! What are you trying to do? Be John Wayne?' He replied, 'Nope, just George Bacon.'

"When we rejoined the rest of the team, we took the left flank where the NVA was the closest. The NVA had laid down a base of fire from the route of our withdrawal

GEORGE WASHINGTON
BACON, III
28 Woolworth Street
Eggsie . . . good-natured . . .
reticent . . . liked by everyone
. . . has brilliance under cover
. . . a man in perpetual motion.

George Bacon's picture in the 1964 Longmeadow (Mass.) High School yearbook. (Private collection of the Bacon family.)

and were trying to envelop us. Suddenly two NVA popped up out of nowhere with their AKs clattering. I hit the dirt but George blasted back. I don't know if he got them, but they quit firing. Finally the Charley Model gunships arrived, but before we lifted off, both the gunships and George and I had expended all our ammo. George was carrying twenty-two twenty-round mags for his CAR and I carried seventeen thirty-six-round mags in four ammo pouches with one in the 'K.'

"George went home in April. I believe he had spent about eighteen months in C&C [Command & Control]. I remember one letter from George that stated he was displeased with the attitudes of most of his college classmates. In the same letter he said he was going to work for 'Christians in Action,' George's personal code for the CIA. George attended agency training in North Carolina, Florida, and Virginia. He wrote once in a while but never said exactly what he was doing."

Another Special Forces trooper who served with Bacon in SOG was Frank McCloskey, who is at present a detective on the Washington, D.C., police homicide squad. McCloskey first met Bacon at Fort Bragg, and when he arrived in Vietnam, he wrangled himself an assignment to Bacon's unit because of their earlier friendship. This was Command & Control North (CCN), Forward Operations Base (FOB) 4, located at Da Nang near Marble Mountain.

It was a highly classified unit that operated under the cover of being a training unit for indigenous forces, Nung mercenaries, and Vietnamese Special Forces volunteers. That was what they told the Marines who were based around the area, although McCloskey says the Marines never really believed it. All pretense of being a training operation ended one day "when we came back with a chopper full of dead Americans and all of our Marine buddies saw them. I think they never really believed we were just training personnel anyhow."

Shortly before McCloskey's arrival at Da Nang, George Bacon had been badly wounded during a North Vietnamese sapper raid on the SF camp, a raid in which seventeen Americans were killed and even more Vietnamese.

Before that, Bacon had been leading SF recon and raiding parties into Laos, the DMZ, and North Vietnam, usually "body snatching" efforts to capture a ranking North Vietnamese officer or rescue American POWs. "George loved that kind of work," McCloskey recalls. But after the sapper raid, American officers in Saigon decided that highly trained SF medics were too valuable to risk as leaders of recon or raiding parties. So Bacon was assigned to the camp dispensary.

"That didn't wash well with George," McCloskey recalls. He loved action and hated communists, and was happier out in the bush fighting them.

"One day I came back from an operation and went looking for George and couldn't find him. People said they hadn't seen him for some time. He'd just disappeared.

"Some of the officers thought he'd deserted, but we all knew George, he wouldn't do anything like that. Finally, we found that he was at Kontum with FOB 2. He had just gone there, sort of taken over and had organized his own combat team of Montagnards [Laotians] and was out in the bush all the time, doing what he liked to do. I got to Kontum a couple of times and looked for George but couldn't find him because he was always out in the bush." McCloskey had no further personal contact with Bacon in Vietnam, although they corresponded then and later and remained close friends.

McCloskey finished his tour in Vietnam, continuing the longrange recon patrols at which the SF units excelled. Often they went out disguised in North Vietnamese uniforms and armed with communist weapons—AK–47s and Tokarev pistols or Uzi submachine guns and silenced .22 caliber semiautomatic pistols.

After leaving Vietnam and the army and returning to the States, Bacon resumed his college education. He enrolled at the University of Massachusetts. But scholastic life was not very exciting.

He was contacted through an old friend from Vietnam by the CIA and was offered a job advising the Meo tribesmen in Northern Laos. Bacon was not satisfied with the situation in Southeast Asia as reported in the newspapers or on television. He accepted the offer. Bacon's father asked him why he was interrupting his education a second time. Bacon replied that the university would always be there but an opportunity with the CIA might not.

He threw himself into the months of intensive training with the agency, as he had with Special Forces. George was assigned to Northern Laos as a case officer. He served as the American counterpart to the Meo General Vang Pao and he roved the Plain of Jars and Skyline Ridge with large Meo combat units in an attempt to contain the North Vietnamese regular units, who were showing up in force.

For more than a decade the agency had been conducting a clandestine war against the communist Pathet Lao and the North Vietnamese on the Plain of Jars. Meo tribesmen, led by General Vang Pao, were armed, trained, and directed by agency case officers, most of whom were veterans of Vietnam. George was responsible for millions of dollars worth of material and for hundreds of thousands of dollars in cash funds. He was promoted three times and was awarded the Intelligence Star (see picture on page 101), the agency's second highest award, for setting an example of leadership for the Meo troops while under fire.

The citation with the medal stated:

> Mr. George W. Bacon III is hereby awarded the Intelligence Star in recognition of his outstanding services performed under conditions of grave personal risk. While serving as an advisor to a large indigenous force in Southeast Asia, the key strategic military base to which he was assigned was subjected to a massive enemy attack. During the four-month siege, Mr. Bacon and his associates handled a myriad of organizational, logistical and tactical problems experienced by the friendly forces. Despite heavy enemy bombardment, Mr. Bacon volunteered to remain on duty at the base providing moral and physical support, thus inspiring the indigenous defenders to withstand the attack. Mr. Bacon's courageous and professional performance was in keeping with the highest tradition of the Agency, reflecting great credit on him and the Federal service.

Another case officer and friend of Bacon's recalled, "I met George early in 1971. One of the things that made George unique was that he was a hard charger. Unlike most of the other case officers who went around armed to the teeth, George walked around most of the time with a .45 pistol, if that. Half the time he forgot the pistol. George railed against the system. Agency policy dictated that case officers were not allowed to participate in combat. George observed neither the spirit nor the letter of the 'law.' He had a penchant for doing things himself, which meant, more or less, leading a lot of these little operations.

"Late in 1972 or early in 1973, our base at Long Tieng was located in a long valley. We extended out miles and miles from there, but eventually we were pushed back to the point where we were on the floor of the valley. One hilltop belonged to friendly troops and one hilltop had enemy troops; we periodically swapped hilltops.

"The hostile forces looked down on our base from a distance of a couple of clicks [kilometers]. There was an operation mounted to retake a strategically important hill using General Yang Pao's crack troops, if you could call any of them crack troops. Anyway, George led this whole thing himself, unbeknownst to the CIA management, of course.

"This was indicative of the way he did things. If he had been caught doing it (well, he's lucky he didn't get his ass shot off), the CIA would have fired him. Or at least they would have shipped him back home. In any case, George was dearly loved by the people he worked with.

"I remember George had a problem with the Air America pilots. He was more aggressive than they were. George was in charge of Site 15, which was manned by one or two battalions of Thai mercenaries. It was surrounded for several months and it was very difficult to get him in and out of there. Both George and his supplies had to fly in and fly out; same with the wounded. The enemy had the site ringed with 12.7mm antiaircraft guns which, of course, made it a little uncomfortable for the chopper pilots. George was constantly at odds with the chopper pilots because he felt they were very highly paid and they should be more aggressive; at least as aggressive as he was. Most of the pilots didn't agree with him.

"George was superenergetic; he used to run all the time. He couldn't wait to get going. He was always one of the first guys up in the morning, and one of the last guys back.

"At Long Tieng, we were under siege several times. Eventually the agency pulled almost all of the Americans out. The guys used to come in in the morning and leave at night. However, there were usually three or four of us in the valley at night. George and another guy, though, were in the valley almost all the time. Most of the other guys were happy to get out at night and go on to Vientiane or Thailand.

"But not George. He was there constantly; months on end. The situation got pretty dicey sometimes; there were a lot of artillery incoming and it could be very uncomfortable. George and this other guy just dug themselves a great big hole in the ground and made a bunker out of it. They just hung in there the whole time." It was for this that the CIA awarded Bacon the Intelligence Star.

Another CIA case officer recalled, "When things were going bad for us in Long Tieng Valley we used to amuse ourselves watching the Kayak through binoculars, walking from one position to another. [Kayak was Bacon's code name in Laos, derived from one of his favorite sports.] He was, in my estimation, and probably in everybody's, one of the best case officers over there. He was a lot more dedicated than at least I was, that's for damn sure. He really never gave up. We'd have long discussions as to the futility of the situation but he never gave up hope. As a matter of fact, he'd get kind of incensed when you'd start talking about it. He had a kind of never-say-die attitude, at least as far as communism was concerned.

"He was always where he really didn't have to be. I remember one time when we were defending a place called Skyline Ridge, he was up in one foxhole with a Laotian colonel and a Thai colonel. When he received a radio message, he jumped out of one foxhole into another. A mortar round came in right where he had been standing and killed one of the colonels. He carried the other one on his back about three miles down the slope. We could see him coming down the slope; he was taking mortar fire all the way down. The enemy forward observers were adjusting mortar fire on him; they had him bracketed for the whole three miles, but he kept plodding on. That's the kind of guy he was.

"I remember another time when the position he was on took a direct hit by a two thousand-pound bomb. One of our 'fast movers' [jets] dropped a 'long round' and it landed right in the middle of Kayak's position. He was with a bunch of Thais and everybody was standing up watching the air strike. It took about two weeks to get all the wounded and dead out of there. Kayak stayed there the whole time though

Bacon (using radio set) calling in artillery fire on enemy positions on the Plain of Jars, Laos. General Vang Pao, leader of the CIA-sponsored Meo tribesmen, is on the left. (Private collection of the Bacon family.)

Bacon (center) and Vang Pao, front right, discuss strategy during a short lunch break. (Private collection of the Bacon family.)

Bacon, on ground with radio, and General Vang Pao, second from right, after firing recoilless rifle at communist units. (Private collection of the Bacon family.)

Bacon, left, was idolized by the Meo enlisted men and stern with incompetent officers. (Private collection of the Bacon family.)

Bacon, with map, and another American CIA officer discuss operations with an Air America chopper pilot. (Private collection of the Bacon family.)

Bacon, center, often disobeyed CIA directives and led combat operations himself against communist forces. (Private collection of the Bacon family.)

Bacon, second from right, with ex-Marine Bart Bonner (center), who founded the Veterans and Volunteers for Vietnam (VVV). (Photo by Robert K. Brown.)

Bacon, shown in his diving suit, graduated first in his class from the Commercial Diving Center in Wilmington, California. (Private collection of the Bacon family.)

he could have gone out with the first helicopter. Another time he was caught in the middle of an Arc Light [B–52] strike. He was again in a place where he didn't have to be, and he was very fortunate.

"Some of the sites were very remote. They were not any less secure than other sites, but they were remote. When you went up there you were locked in for two or three months at a crack. It was a very undesirable assignment. He was the type of individual who always volunteered for stuff like that.

"The indigenous commanders didn't much care for him because he always expected them to do their damn job, where the rest of us would try to get along instead of pushing them. The indigenous enlisted men liked the hell out of him because he was always right there. He'd flat tell a commander to his face that he was incompetent. He just kind of spelled it out like it was."

It was a very difficult period but Bacon's letters home demonstrated sensitivity and a desire to keep the family at ease.

> "27 May 1971
> I was really glad to hear that at last after I guess about a year of searching you found a house that meets all of the specifications required.
> I'd like to ask you if you can to dig up and carry back to Massachusetts my English Walnut Trees (two of them) and my Chinese Chestnut Trees (two of them) and possibly the plum tree, if it can be moved without the new owners caring too much. The other four trees are in a pretty inconspicuous position and it shouldn't be noticed that they are gone. And how about a fence to keep our dogs and other dogs out of the pond that you are going to build. Is such a thing possible or desirable?"

> "8 July 1971
> We've had a month of good weather and I've been working hard again. Seven days a week from 0700 til 2030 when the meeting is finally over. Now today we've finally gotten a break because of some real bad weather which has moved in on our area and no aircraft can take off or land. So I'm using this opportunity to write to you while I am not real tired.…
> I was real glad to hear that you got the trees planted all right and that the dogs like the new place. And especially that you will be able to make a new pond."

> "10 September 1971
> I'm not taking any time off or trips for many reasons. First, I really do like the Meo People and it is good to know that they depend on me for certain things and that I can do something to help them, plus it is good being outdoors all day and this area is very beautiful."

During Bacon's last months in Laos it became apparent that there would be a negotiated settlement to the conflict. Bacon knew that he would have to leave but he felt that he had not completed his task. He wanted to improve the lot of the Laotians with whom he had been serving. He set up a sawmill, perhaps the only one in the country, which years afterwards was still in operation. He also established a cattle ranch and a pig farm, and he built two schools.

Bacon left a lasting impression on the people with whom he worked. After he had left Laos, his American CIA supervisor in that country wrote him the following letter:

16 Oct 73
Long Tieng

"Kayak,

I've tried about fifteen times this morning to write you a letter … each feeble attempt has turned out to be stilted and artificial, so I'm trying again to turn out a brief and honest communication that will simply let you know that you are missed, and that those of us here who worked with you have not forgotten. [Name deleted] left your letter with me when he left for Missoula, and I have read it a number of times … each time marveling at its eloquence and sincerity.

"I knew you could write … having your colorful dispatches from Bouam Long . . . but never dreamed that you were a 'writer' … ever considered doing it for a living? You'd make a marvelous war correspondent, and should be somewhere east of Suez this very minute. For Christ's sake, change your major to journalism and get with it! All that boundless energy and creative talent should not be wasted on a pedestrian career … go spend it, and yourself, somewhere where it will do some good … not all journalists are opportunistic assholes, you know. Kipling was a correspondent, also Mark Twain and Winston Churchill … to name but a few of the best. God, what a challenge! You could make it, George and we who 'knew you when' would be so damned proud …

"I'm writing an end-of-tour report in which you are mentioned as one of the four best Case Officers to serve in Long Tieng during the period '67–'73.… (Not that my opinion of you will be of any importance to you … just mentioning it in passing.) VP [Vang Pao] mentions you often … almost daily … and your memory with these people is assured. If you accomplish nothing else of value in your life (which I refuse to believe) you will always have that … you were where you were needed at the time you were needed most … never mind that nobody will ever know it but yourself and a few that were with you.

"Good luck to you, George … wherever you go and whatever you do. It was a privilege and a pleasure to have worked with you.—Mu Zjong Nuh."

After Laos, Bacon returned home and resumed his study of political science at the University of Massachusetts. He graduated *summa cum laude* in June, 1974.

His father recalled, "When George was a student at the University of Massachusetts he sprained his ankle while sport parachute jumping, but he had promised to run a relay race (vets versus students), and despite his injury he ran the race. As it turned out, the foot was broken and had to have a cast put on it. Even with the cast, George came in fourth in the race. When George got back from having the cast put on, he explained that he knew the doctor was young and inexperienced and that the cast was not properly set. So George broke the cast with a hatchet and put another one on himself."

Bacon was not a person obsessed solely with fighting communism. Among other things, he was an ardent naturalist. He would often go to the ocean or to wildlife sanctuaries to photograph birds. He was interested in ecology and organic gardening.

His father recalled that Bacon could often be found at Washington parties off in a corner explaining the ins and outs of a compost pile to someone.

Just before the fall of Saigon in April, 1975, Bacon wanted to return to fight alongside the Vietnamese who still resisted the Viet Cong, The most expeditious means of achieving this seemed to be to contact Bart Bonner, head of Veterans and Volunteers for Vietnam. Bonner, ex-Marine and Vietnam vet, had been owner of a telephone answering service in a small town in upstate New York. He went to Washington to establish the VVV with the objective of recruiting personnel to return to Saigon and fight the NVA in the waning days of the Nguyen Van Thieu regime. Bacon offered Bonner his assistance.

Bonner recollects, "We hit it off right away. He was enthusiastic and competent. We chose him to organize the military aspect of our effort. He was strong, honest and dedicated to the cause … just a fantastic person."

According to Bonner, Bacon felt that the U.S. had betrayed the peoples of Southeast Asia; that the government and the Congress had "betrayed their word of honor." Bonner was aware that Bacon had worked for the agency in Laos, but stated that he was close-mouthed about his current connection with them. Bacon was now learning Cambodian and was scheduled for an assignment in Cambodia prior to the fall of Phnom Penh.

In a letter to SOF publisher Robert K. Brown, dated October 16, 1975, George said, "Don't be shocked by the connection I had with the CIA—when I was working with Bart on the VVV, I was doing that completely on my own and, at first, without their knowledge. It's illegal for government employees to engage in political activities, thus the Agency took an especially dim view of my connection with such an explosive and renegade outfit as VVV. I was going to resign from the Agency anyway, because I couldn't get back to Southeast Asia with them."

In another letter to Brown, dated September 29, 1975, George is responding to Brown's suggestion that the VVV be reorganized as a clearinghouse providing information on opportunities to fight communism, and that it be renamed Veterans and Volunteers for Freedom. George states, "… I have seen no opportunity existing at present that would be suitable for the injection of a force of American volunteers with the possible exception of Angola. I feel from my own limited reading of the scant news available, that Angola is the only area today where American volunteers could be employed to fight communism, and that your magazine could be an excellent way to spread the good word about this opportunity."

Bacon spent two months with the VVV and, after their efforts terminated, attended the Commercial Diving Center at Wilmington, California, where he completed an advanced course in skin and scuba diving, air and mixed gas diving, and underwater photography. While completing diving school, Bacon authored "The Challenge of Deep Sea Diving," an article published in *Soldier of Fortune*. After graduating first in his class, he worked for a diving firm in Louisiana, then flew to England where he unsuccessfully attempted to sign on with oil firms operating in the North Sea.

Then, in early December, 1975, he flew to South Africa. He wanted to do a photojournalism piece on the situation in Angola, where Cuban troops were helping the leftist MPLA (Popular Movement for the Liberation of Angola) seize control of the country. The journalistic project, however, did not pan out.

Bacon then went to Lusaka, Zambia, where he offered his services to Dr. Jonas Savimbi's UNITA (National Union for the Total Independence of Angola), one of the anticommunist groups fighting the MPLA. Some of Savimbi's lieutenants were receptive to Bacon's overtures, but when Bacon met with Savimbi's number two man he was turned away with no explanation. Undaunted, Bacon returned to the United States and in January linked up with a group of blacks who were supposedly recruiting for Angola and who were sponsored by the Congress for Racial Equality (CORE). After a while, however, it became evident that nothing would come of this effort.

Bonner, who met Bacon and members of the SOF staff in D.C. on February 4, 1976, commented, "George felt the CORE people were phony. Everybody was 'Colonel-this' or 'Captain-that.' Everyone went out and bought eleven-dollar red berets. He initially thought that somebody might have something going, but there was no money. He dug into his own pocket for the phone deposit and to buy food.

Consequently, Bacon and Bonner phoned David Bufkin, selfstyled recruiter for the FNLA (National Front for the Liberation of Angola, another anticommunist group), and discovered that he was planning to leave for Angola. During their trip to New York to meet Bufkin, the two men decided that Bacon would offer to organize an effective recruiting program in the United States for the FNLA, as it appeared that Bufkin's operation was slipshod and disorganized.

Commented Bonner later, "Bufkin obviously had no funds available. He operated out of motels. He had no office. Potential recruits had to pay their own travel expenses. It was definitely a shoestring operation. You couldn't expect men to pay their own way over there. Our plan was to offer to provide the FNLA with as many qualified men as we could if they would guarantee $1,000 for each man recruited. We then would pay everything—open an office, pay for the recruits' plane fare and expenses while we processed them, etc. It would have been a strictly nonprofit deal, as one-way airfare was $700."

Bufkin said on the phone that there were already between one hundred and fifty and two hundred Americans in Angola and that the anticommunist forces had plenty of weapons. It turned out that neither of these statements was correct.

Bonner described the meeting of Bacon and himself with Bufkin: "We met Bufkin and the other recruits at the Air France terminal in Kennedy Airport. No means of identifying Bufkin had been agreed upon, so we just looked around and picked him out. Bufkin was wearing big sunglasses and cowboy boots. We just went over and asked him who he was.

"I got one look at Bufkin and said to George, 'We've got a loser,' and he replied, 'You're right.'

"The other six or seven Americans were all walking around playing superspy, like nobody was supposed to recognize anybody else. They weren't even cool enough to buy tickets to Brussels; they had all gotten tickets for Zaire.

"George later called me from Kinshasa confirming his arrival, and said that he had talked to the FNLA leaders but they were not willing to organize a formal recruiting program in the U.S. because they claimed they were unable to fund it.

"He advised me not to encourage others to go over, as the situation did not seem to be on the 'up and up.' Anyone that did come over should be professional and experienced."

Bonner later stated, "The Africans just used George and the rest. They had nothing to fight the Cuban tanks with. Their own people weren't fighting. I had a feeling when I saw Bufkin that it was a bum operation. I told George not to do anything that would endanger him—just get in, look around, and get out.

"I think if George had been told the truth he wouldn't have gone. He was expecting to go over there and find an active company of Americans. Instead he went over there and found about half-a-dozen men trying to stop a Cuban armada."

Despite his doubts, Bacon plunged into the Angolan situation in the way he knew best: as a fighting man. Michael T. Sharpley, a former English paratrooper who served four years with the Territorial Reserves and was a veteran of the Rhodesian Army, met Bacon on February 12, 1976, in Angola. Sharpley recalled, "George was a fireball. Once he made contact with the FNLA forces and arrived at the base at San Salvador, there was no stopping him; he really went to town. Bacon and the other Yanks equipped themselves to leave for the bush on the day they arrived.

"The next time I saw Bacon he was mining a bridge. Gary Acker [one of the Americans], myself, and the rest of a patrol left Quimba Junction about a half hour after first light. On our way to San Salvador we met up with Bacon and an Englishman and about six Africans.

"There were two flat concrete bridges. George had dug two trenches, one at either end of the first bridge. He packed it out with five pounds of TNT. I assisted with setting the charges; the fuses were already set and run back, so we packed earth on top of the bridge and ran Land Rovers back and forth over it. The mining of one bridge was complete. We stopped work and had a skimpy breakfast. Afterward our patrol left and went on to San Salvador, leaving Bacon and the others to mine the second bridge.

"On our way to San Salvador, we met another patrol coming from the opposite direction going to Quimba. Both patrols stopped and Acker crossed from our jeep to the other that was heading toward Quimba.

"Our patrol reached San Salvador at about 3:00 in the afternoon. It was then that we learned that the vast Cuban strength was only four miles away. Upon hearing the news, we evacuated San Salvador and reached Zaire about three days later."

It was now February 14, 1976, and Bacon and Acker heard of the patrol that had not returned on schedule. With his usual enthusiasm and energy George armed himself, secured the Land Rover, and set off at once to search for them. He was not to return alive.

An account of Bacon's death is contained in a deposition purportedly given by Gary Martin Acker, twenty-one, a Marine veteran of Vietnam and a mercenary who, at the time of Bacon's death, was riding in the Land Rover with him. Acker suffered a leg wound in the ambush, was captured, and is now serving a sixteen-year jail sentence in Angola.

The deposition was given by Acker to Robert E. Cesner Jr., a Columbus, Ohio attorney who represented Acker and Gearhart at their trial in Angola. It was read over the phone to George Baeon III's father while a reporter listened on an extension taking notes. It was read by Ed Fugit, a country officer for Africa in the State Department in Washington. It was the first time George Bacon's father had heard it. It was about seven months after his son's death.

(The "affiant" is Acker and, according to the senior Bacon, the age listed at the time of death is wrong):

> Statement, July 2m Luanda, Angola: The undersigned, Gary Martin Acker, being first duly cautioned and sworn, deposes and says as follows:
>
> Affiant was acquainted with and knew one George Bacon, an American citizen, 27 years of age, having an identifying scar on the right side of chest. Affiant met said George Bacon en route to Kinshasa, Zaire, and from there associated with him in the country of Angola.
>
> On Feb. 14, 1976, affiant was with said George Bacon in Angola, Gbmba, when he witnessed said George Bacon mortally wounded by gunfire in an immediate proximity to affiant; said wound being multiple and in the chest and abdominal area, and that said death occurred at approximately 12 P.M., Angola time, Feb. 14, 1976; that the body of the deceased was transferred in a truck with and in the presence of the affiant for several hours; that the body of the deceased evidenced no signs of life, and that George Bacon was deceased. Further affiant saith not.
>
> Signed by Acker, witnessed by Cesner and one other. Sworn to and subscribed in my presence this first day of July, 1976.

The one major mystery surrounding Bacon is, "What, if any, were his connections with the CIA prior to and during his presence in Angola?" As Bruce McCabe wrote in a feature article on Bacon in the September 26, 1976 issue of the *Boston Sunday Globe*, "Some people feel that George Bacon, who had been an honored agent with the CIA before going to Angola, was with the Agency, or acting at its behest in some capacity, at the time of his death. They feel that the secrecy and disinterest which surround Bacon's death in some areas of Washington, particularly on Capitol Hill, represent an attempt to separate Bacon from the country whose ideals he venerated, an attempt to isolate or "discredit" him as just another soldier of fortune."

During January and early February, 1976, Bacon had worked with a group of blacks in the Washington, D.C., area, sponsored by the leadership of CORE, who were recruiting personnel to serve with the pro-Western forces in Angola. Bacon told his old comrade-in-arms who lived in the area, Frank McCloskey, just before he went to Angola that he was back "on the Company payroll" and was going to Angola to "check out the mercenaries." McCloskey believes that the agency was puzzled about the mercenary operation, wasn't sure who was recruiting or bankrolling them, and wanted to know. Bacon was a logical man to send to penetrate the mercenary operation and find out.

"I am absolutely sure that George was not over there as a pure and simple mercenary as such," McCloskey says. "If George had found an opportunity to make a good buck just by doing something we were both good at, I know he would have contacted me and invited me to get in on the action. I am certain of that. George always got in touch with me when he was going to do anything that sounded exciting and challenging. I think he was working for the Company, trying to check out the mercenary operation and just got caught up in circumstances."

Shortly after Bacon's death, Ernie Volkman, fifteen-year veteran national security affairs correspondent for *Newsday* and contributor to the *Los Angeles Times-Washington Post* news service, became interested in Bacon's CIA ties. The well-connected Volkman queried personnel in the director's office at agency headquarters in Langley, Virginia. He was greeted by a stone wall: George Bacon never had a connection with the CIA. Volkman recalls, "On 4 December 1975, I wrote an article for the *LA Times* alleging that a covert CIA airlift to Angola from Zaire coincided with two brigades of Cubans entering Angola. Two days later, the Agency convened a private briefing to refute my story. But two weeks later, Angola [CIA] Station Chief John Stockwell made public his lengthy resignation letter, in which he cited mercenary recruitment by the Agency and its general mishandling of the Angola situation as a major cause. This caused the Agency to admit publicly that they were running a $20 million operation in Angola.

"The whole CIA-Angola situation was very confusing. Every time I mentioned Bacon's name, there was a great deal of scurrying and contradiction and nervousness."

But after *Soldier of Fortune* magazine published a eulogy to Bacon in the fall of 1976, Volkman's eyebrows rose along with his blood pressure. Not only was Bacon known to the Agency, he'd been a case officer for over four years and had received their second highest award, the Intelligence Star. Armed with this information, Volkman again confronted his Agency source, who then regrouped and allowed that Bacon had indeed worked for the Agency, but had resigned prior to entering Angola. Volkman, wise to Agency ways, knew "resignations" were a standard method of disowning compromised operatives. A resignation may be filled out by an agent at any time and filed for safekeeping. If it becomes necessary to cut the agent loose; the resignation is dated appropriately and used as evidence. Thus, Volkman thinks Bacon was still employed by the Agency while in Angola. Whether or not George Bacon was under the Agency's aegis when he died, it will not bring him back to life.

If you can tell a man by his books, so too can you intuit a great deal by a man's favorite quotations, and Bacon had many.

From General Douglas MacArthur (1962): "Yours is the profession of arms ... the will to win ... the sure knowledge that in war there is no substitute for victory, that if you lose, the nation will be destroyed, the very obsession of your public service must be duty, honor, country."

And from John F. Kennedy: "Whether they wish us well or ill, let every nation know ... that we shall pay any price, bear any burden, meet any hardship, support any friend, oppose any foe to assure the survival and success of liberty. This much we pledge and more."

George Washington Bacon III had fulfilled this promise and paid the final price.

CHAPTER 9

David Bufkin: Seller of Soldiers

From commercial crop duster to mercenary recruiter to soldier of fortune—an espionage soldier of fortune—that appears to be the factual side of David Bufkin's career. Most is obscured in a haze of mystery where truth blends with rumor and separation of the two is just about impossible. But mystery makes mystique, and the mystique of Bufkin distinguishes him from other mercenaries. "Cuban spy, double agent, CIA informant, self-styled mere recruiter for Angola and Zaire—who is the real David Bufkin?" asked *Soldier of Fortune* magazine.

Esquire a few years ago reported that Bufkin was "uncomfortable" because of the "legal ramifications of his recruiting, his various covert activities in recent years that involved foreign governments and this [U.S.] one, and certain sinister organized domestic elements. And there was his military past."

Bufkin, it appears, always wanted to be a combat soldier. Said *Esquire*: "He lied about his age to enlist in the army in 1953, was discovered and booted out, then proceeded to enlist fraudulently three more times. He volunteered persistently for Vietnam duty but was never sent there. His frustration led to trouble during each enlistment—assault and battery, disobeying a direct order, going AWOL. Each of his four discharges was less than satisfactory."

Said Bufkin, "I got along great with the guys, and even sometimes with my commanding officers. I just can't explain it. I'm just not the soldier-of-the-month type. Out of eight years altogether, I give 'em a total of about one bad year. Hell, I spent more time in the stockade than most people spend in the fucking Army."

Bufkin's "odd job soldier-of-fortune" activities, reported *Esquire*, included "moving arms and people in and out of the country, stealing things for various companies, delivering unregistered, decommissioned military planes to foreign countries and … 'procuring' some sophisticated foreign-made military equipment for a U.S. government agency that wanted to examine it."

Bufkin made "good money" (about $24,000 in the best year) but decided he could do even better in the business of recruiting mercenaries for clients. He said, "I wanted to be like the big recruiters in Europe. There are two or three who have files on all kinds of highly qualified specialists. You want to blow a hole in a Russian ship, they can supply specialists who will draw up the plan, underwater demolition divers, equipment, everything. I wanted to be the American connection. Right now in the United States there may not be more than thirty or forty mercs with a few years of experience. I was going to set up a file of maybe five hundred men, like those big shots in Europe."

The war was on in Angola. Bufkin went to Africa, made the necessary contacts, and then began recruiting mercenaries. He arranged for five men to go to Angola: one Argentine and four Americans, including George Bacon. That effort ended in tragedy. The war ended with the victory of the Cubansupported leftist forces, and the Canadian and Bacon were killed in action, the Argentine and one of the other Americans were captured and imprisoned, and the third American, Daniel Gearhart, was executed.

Bufkin has described the final days of the group and his own participation in their activities.

"… George Bacon went out to a bridge, about fifteen kilometers south of San Salvador, and put satchel charges on the pillars and so forth. He didn't blow the bridge because we didn't know the exact position of the enemy, and we had a small T–34 tank and an armored car, and we didn't know if we were going to need the bridge ourselves.

"The same night, a reconnaissance patrol went out south of the bridge. The next morning another patrol went out. I was flying back and forth in a Cessna 172 recon. I gave word back that there was a large column of one hundred armored vehicles, plus approximately fifteen hundred to two thousand Cuban troops, with T–54 tanks, moving up the road north toward the bridge.

"Now, Bacon went back out to the bridge that morning to blow it. He had my report and apparently—nobody can know for sure—he blew the bridge and then went on south to try to warn the two recon patrols. It was a very courageous thing to do. I flew over the bridge, but it was under cover of large trees and I couldn't see it at all. But the armored column was all bunched up at the south end, so the bridge must have been blown.

"A little earlier, before Bacon blew the bridge, Gearhart and [Gary] Acker were returning from the night recon patrol, and they met the morning patrol going out. The morning patrol didn't have any automatic weapons, so Gearhart took his machine gun and mounted it on the Land Rover with the morning patrol, and he and Acker went back out with them, headed south. That's who Bacon was going to warn."

Bacon and Acker did not make it. They were ambushed. Bacon was killed and Acker captured.

During the last hours Bufkin kept flying: "I was in the airplane every minute, back and forth, even sleeping in the thing. But I couldn't find anybody."

It was the capture and imprisonment in Angloa of three of his mercenaries that evidently led Bufkin into the murky world of espionage. In an effort to obtain information about the two men Bufkin made contact with an official of the Cuban embassy in Mexico City. According to Bufkin: "I approached him at the Aztec Hotel and I told him that it wasn't for myself, but I was trying to find out all the information I could about Gary Acker because of a concerned father heartbroken mother and that type of thing. He says, 'we'll see what we can do and we'll get back to you,' so that's how it all started."

It appears that at this meeting Bufkin made an offer to spy for the Cubans, perhaps in return for information about the imprisoned mercenaries or perhaps with their eventual release in mind.

Why would the Cubans trust a person who had been involved in the side opposing them in Angola? Bufkin figured: "I was well known as a mercenary in Angola. There were a lot of newspaper stories … that didn't present me in blue-blooded light. In other words, I was out for hire … Some people had the impression that I would have worked for the [Cuban-supported] MPLA had they hired me first."

Subsequently Bufkin received a phone call from a Mr. Rodríguez, Cuba's consul-general in Montreal, Canada, asking Bufkin to come to Montreal for a meeting. Bufkin was instructed to be at the consulate on September 6—the year was 1976—because that day was a Canadian holiday and the consulate would be closed. Bufkin has described his visit.

"I was told to go up to the gate, ring the buzzer, identify myself as 'Dave' from California and then the gate would be opened. It's an electrical gate. And I did [what I was told to do]. I walked up to the box that hangs on the gate, said this is 'Dave from California' and the gate swung open. I walked in, went to the receptionist and she took me back into the consulate, and then I went into an office and met Rodríguez and another cohort of his."

Bufkin was questioned by Rodríguez about Acker and Gus Grillo, the imprisoned mercenaries. And he was also questioned about the Angolan anticommunist guerrilla organization, the FNLA. The Cubans were particularly interested in an ordnance warehouse maintained by the FNLA in Kinshasa, Zaire, where Bufkin had once bunked. Rodríguez and Bufkin discussed the possibility of blowing up the warehouse.

The Cubans wanted, Bufkin felt, "to see just how far I would go and how much I would tell them … to see if I could be trusted. The [other] individual that was in the room … I never spoke to the man, he never opened his mouth, but I was under the impression that he is a lot higher than Rodríguez and Rodríguez was pretty high in the espionage network in Montreal."

Bufkin returned to his home in Kerman, California, to await further word from the Cubans. It came in the form of another call from Rodríguez, who stated: "The answer is positive. They [presumably Cuban intelligence headquarters in Havana] are interested in business." Bufkin was told to return to Montreal. The Cubans would pay his fare and expenses.

Bufkin went back to Montreal and there negotiated the terms under which he would work for the Cubans. He asked for money and for the release of Acker and Grillo. The Cuban said they could not effect the release of the mercenaries but they agreed to pay Bufkin. His mission would be to gather intelligence only. He received an initial payment of $1,000 and then additional sums of money. He was given a short course in espionage techniques, as well as detailed microfilm instructions on how to establish contact with Cuban intelligence in Kinshasa and later back in Montreal. The instructions for Kinshasa were as follows:

"Kinshasa, Zaire: The Place: Central post office, 30th of June Ave. You must be standing on the sidewalk at the entrance of the second row of post office boxes from right to left. Time: 1200 hours local time. You should hold a canvas painting of the type usually sold in the Kinshasa market in your right hand. Our representative will be near you in the third row or corridor of post office boxes. He will have a red book under his left arm and will be smoking a cigar. You should not approach him. Once visual contact has been established, follow him. He will drop an empty cigarette box. Pick it up and follow the instructions you will find inside. The date of this meeting: last Saturday in October. The reserve dates: first Saturday in November and the second Saturday in November. Information requested: name of CIA personnel involved, frequency used in ground and air communications, the codes, type of transmitter, infiltration plans in Angola, military operations with details: number of men, type of weapons, names of Americans serving with the FNLA, operational zones, agents inside Angola, sources of support in Angola, points of infiltration, arms deposits in Angola held by the FNLA, source of income, information on CIA air operations from Lusaka [Zambia], recruitment procedures, number of nationalities, salaries, morale, morale of the black troops, acceptance among the black FNLA or do you need to have white mercenaries, relations between FNLA and UNITA at its top level, discrepancies of joint military operations."

Bufkin taped some of his conversations with Rodríguez and he also maintained contact with the FBI and CIA. On a trip to Washington, he has said, he "reported to the FBI," whose agents "debriefed me for one day." As for the CIA Bufkin has thus described his relationship: "When I first made contact with the Cubans I told an individual that I know that it is in the CIA that I had made contact and established an appointment with him [Rodríguez] in Montreal and that I was going to leave. He says, 'Dave, now I can't tell you to do this, but I'm not going to tell you not to do this, but if you do it, be damn sure to stay in touch with us, let us know what flight you are leaving on, what flight you are going to arrive on, what time and where you are going to.' "

Bufkin flew to Kinshasa and there was picked up by an FNLA representative. He was taken to the headquarters of the leader of the guerrilla organization, Holden

David Bufkin (right), about whom little is known and much is speculated. (Private collection of Robert K. Brown.)

Roberto. Bufkin has described his arrival: "... [I] reported in to the FNLA and they were expecting me. The CIA had already informed them that I was coming and I stayed ... two or three days and made my meeting downtown at the post office building. That meeting was covered by the FNLA, the CIA and probably [Zaire President Sese Seko] Mobutu's secret police."

Bufkin spotted the Cuban agent at the post office and, in accord with the procedure described in the microfilm, the agent dropped a cigarette box. Inside this were further instructions directing Bufkin to go to the Inter-Continental Hotel. He went to the hotel and ordered a drink at the bar and waited. The Cuban agent came in and they talked. Having been briefed beforehand, Bufkin informed the agent about a small FNLA arms cache in Angola which consisted of M–2 carbines and a few thousand rounds of ammunition. He also told of supposed infiltration plans and he reported that FNLA morale was "good." The information was not much but was primarily intended to establish Bufkin's credibility. The meeting lasted about fifteen minutes.

Although he may have convinced the Cuban agent, Bufkin knew that his work in Zaire was over: "When I got back to the FNLA I felt that my assignment was finished. The CIA is not supposed to be there. The FNLA is not supposed to be there. They're supposed to be gone and finished, and Mobutu is supposed to have expelled all mercenaries and all guerrillas, et cetera, et cetera. So I came home, thinking I was finished. I had no reason to give an explanation to the Cubans why I left."

Before leaving Africa, however, Bufkin phoned the Special Branch—intelligence organization—in Rhodesia and informed them about two Cuban agents he had seen in Montreal who, Rodríguez had carelessly told Bufkin, were heading for Rhodesia. Special Branch was, naturally, interested in Bufkin's information and he was given another phone number and directed to call "Major Rickson at Peacock Enterprises."

Said Bufkin: "So I called him up and he said, 'Dave, he says, do you think you could come and work with us?' And I told him, gee, I don't know but I'll see, but I have to have something ... to show some credibility that I can work with you."

Bufkin returned to Montreal to resume contact with Rodríguez. To make the contact Bufkin followed the instructions on the microfilm he had been given:

"Place: Canada, Montreal. Mont Royal Station beside telephone at main exit. Time: 1400 hours. Visible signals for ID: Newsweek magazine in left hand. Watchword: Are you Rose Marie's husband? My watchword: Yes, I am. To call a meeting, send a wire to our office with the following text: 'I am planning a trip to Cuba. Please send information on visa requirements.' Use code name 'Clinch.' The meeting will take place on the third day after the date of the wire. Sign it with your code name and code address. There will be two consecutive days reserved for the contact."

Bufkin met with the Cubans and suggested that he perform additional services for them, this time in Rhodesia. They were interested but wanted proof that Bufkin could produce any worthwhile information. The Rhodesian Special Branch sent Bufkin a letter stating that he had been appointed a flight lieutenant in the Rhodesian Air Force. This letter convinced the Cubans that he could obtain military information.

Bufkin spent a week and a half in Montreal, receiving additional instruction. Eight other individuals were also being trained or briefed by Cuban intelligence. Said Bufkin, "none of us stayed together. Our classes were separate. We weren't allowed to socialize. The reason for this was that if I did know them and I got picked up, and had my fingernails pulled out, why, I'm going to tell who the rest of the tribe is. So, that's one reason why we weren't allowed to get to know each other. The second reason is that one of us could be a phony, which in this case, there was."

The "phony," of course, was Bufkin himself.

Bufkin's task in Rhodesia was to obtain intelligence information. "My mission in Rhodesia was to find out the names and addresses of all U.S. ex-military personnel, as many as possible, serving with the Rhodesian forces. It was going to be used as propaganda—mercenaries being hired out of the U.S., to serve with Rhodesian forces. They wanted to know the type of air-to-ground communication that the Rhodesians were using and how many and what type of aircraft were available. They also wanted an estimate of the morale of the black troopers in the Rhodesian African Rifles."

By this time Bufkin and Rodríguez had become good friends. Bufkin related: "Rodríguez took a liking to me. I don't know why—maybe because I'd listen to his scuttlebutt. He liked to show off his spy equipment. For one thing, he carried his documents around in a small, heavy metal case. It was about six inches wide, an inch thick and probably seven inches long. The entire top came off and it had a locking device at the top. The inside of this case was wired up to a small battery and the wires went to solid oxygen or something. I'm not sure what it was, but he could take the top of this case and just twist it, and everything inside the case would burn and disintegrate. I don't know how it worked. He also showed me a Berreta automatic that he carried, and some microfilm that he was carrying for some other individuals—stuff like that. I just happened to listen to him and I guess that's the reason he took a liking to me."

Bufkin flew to Salisbury, Rhodesia's capital, and met with Special Branch agents. They debriefed him on what he had learned in Montreal regarding Cuban intelligence activities. They also showed him a stack of photographs of persons, and Bufkin evidently was able to pick out photos of the two agents he had seen in Montreal who were heading for Rhodesia. These two men had been under surveillance by the Rhodesians, who had allowed them to join the Rhodesian army. But then, alarmed, perhaps because of the arrest of other cuban agents, the two had deserted and possibly fled to neighboring Botswana.

Bufkin bas related that he was instructed by Special Branch to go to Botswana to try to identify positively the two agents/ deserters. He went there but was unable to locate his Rhodesian contact in that country.

Bufkin returned to the States. He had worked as a double agent in Canada, Zaire, Rhodesia, and Botswana. But for now, at least, his career as an espionage soldier of fortune was over.

On Sunday, January 9, 1977, the story of Bufkin's spy activities broke in the Salisbury *Sunday Mail*.

On Monday the Canadian government ordered four Cubans to leave the country, including Rodríguez, and ordered that a fifth diplomat who was out of Canada at the time not return. Three of the Cubans were banned for "conduct incompatible with their status in Canada," and the other two for engaging in subversive activities. Information provided by Bufkin to the CIA and presumably funneled on to the Royal Canadian Mounted Police was a significant factor in exposing the Cuban intelligence apparatus.

Cuba admitted the existence of the spy organization. On January 13, 1977, the Montreal *Gazette* carried the headline, "Havana Defends School of Spies at Consulate," and a story which stated: "The Cuban government yesterday defended using Montreal as a recruiting base to groom spies and four Cubans were expelled from Canada under heavy security for their part in the operation. In an official statement issued through an embassy in Ottawa, the Castro regime, for the first time, admitted the existence of the spy training school here, but stressed the activites of the Montreal consulate had only been directed against the revolutionary National Front for Liberation of Angola."

Bufkin's career as a spy might be over but the danger to him was not. The Dirección General de Inteligencia, Cuba's spy service, like other spy services looks unkindly on people who trick it.

Bufkin, according to his account, was contacted by a Cuban agent he had known in Mexico. The agent arranged to visit Bufkin at his home in Kerman. Related Bufkin: "He was still a little perplexed as to how the whole thing got busted, and they didn't know just how much I really did know. They didn't know how much I had actually told anybody, the CIA or the FBI. And so he, they, wanted to know how much I had told, how much I had said, and how much I really knew. He came down to find out, and we had a confrontation and I didn't quite have the right answers for him.... Everything was pointing directly at me. And I was trying to get out from under it. At the time, I wasn't prepared to answer the questions. The answers that I was giving weren't sufficient."

The discussion between Bufkin and the agent was heated and "we began to play war games." Said Bufkin: "He shot me. We were struggling at first, and he had me on my back and shot me through the left arm, and I pulled my gun and shot him in the center of the chest."

Both men survived.

But today, wherever he goes and whatever he does, David Bufkin must always look over his shoulder and be very careful indeed.

CHAPTER 10

Two in Nicaragua:
William Walker and Mike Echanis

American fighting men have played significant roles in Nicaragua throughout most of its history. Nicaragua was the scene of operations for a famous American soldier of fortune, William Walker.

Walker was born in Nashville in 1824 and studied law and medicine, aiming for a professional career. But he sought excitement, and in 1850 he headed for frontier California. In 1853 he led a small band of adventurers into Mexico's Lower California and declared the establishment of an independent republic. Walker was imprisoned, managed to escape, and fled back to California.

In Nicaragua there existed at this time a bitter rivalry between the cities of Leon and Granada, strongholds of the Liberal and Conservative parties respectively. The Liberals asked Walker to assist them in their feud with the Conservatives, and in 1855 he set out with an expeditionary force of fifty-eight men. Commodore Cornelius Vanderbilt had established a transit company in Nicaragua to enable would-be prospectors to cross the country en route to the gold rush in California. Walker's men seized one of Vanderbilt's steamers on Lake Nicaragua, sailed over, and captured Granada.

Walker, a little man weighing about one hundred pounds, made himself commander-in-chief of the Nicaraguan army and then in 1856 he was "elected" president of the country. He did well and his government was even recognized by the United States. Vanderbilt, however, was an unforgiving sort, and he stirred up other Central Americans into warring on the Yankee usurper. Several hundred additional soldiers of fortune had joined Walker's army, but the army was no match for the Costa Ricans and others who were fighting it. In May, 1857, Walker gave himself into the custody of an American naval officer and returned to the States.

But Walker was a persistent sort. On November 25, 1857, he landed another expedition in Nicaragua. He was less successful than the first time, however, and he was captured and deported. In August, 1860, he tried his luck in another Central American country: this time it was Honduras. And this time he was captured by the British navy and turned over to the Hondurans. Being less understanding than the Nicaraguans, the Hondurans stood Walker before a firing squad on September 12, 1860, and executed him. His luck had run out.

American meddling in Nicaraguan affairs did not by any means end with Walker. There were various political and financial interventions by the United States, and then in July, 1912, American warships landed Marines there. For nineteen of the twenty-one years that followed, American Marines remained in Nicaragua. They organized and trained an indigenous *Guardia Nacional*, and when the Marines finally pulled out on January 2, 1933, the *Guardia* became the military power in the country. And the commander of the *Guardia*, General Anastasio "Tacho" Somoza, was the power behind the government. After three years he tired of being the power *behind* the government and decided to become *the* government. The incumbent president was ousted and "Tacho" had himself elected to the executive office. A political dynasty then began that lasted until 1979.

Over the years there were occasional minor revolts; always the *Guardia* quelled these. On January 10, 1978, Pedro Joaquin Chamorro, a newspaper publisher and outspoken foe of the Somoza family, was ambushed and murdered in Managua. Running the country at the time was President Anastasio Somoza, West Point–trained son of the first "Tacho." (Somoza Two was "Tachito" while his father was alive, and became "Tacho" when his father died. Somoza Two's elder son, also Anastasio, is now "Tachito.")

Although there was no evidence that Somoza had arranged Chamorro's death, this killing set in motion a period of growing turbulence directed against Somoza's government. The cutting edge was the Sandinistas, a clandestine guerrilla group named for a guerrilla chieftain, General Augusto Cesar Sandino, who years earlier had fought the Marines in Nicaragua.

As trouble simmered and flared in Nicaragua in 1978, on the scene in a key spot was a flamboyant American, Michael D. Echanis.

Born on November 16, 1950, Echanis was reared in Ontario, Oregon, a farm community of about 6,500 people on the Snake River. His mother Pat was a homemaker and his father Frank for twenty years ran Plaza's Tavern, a bar with a pool table and a place for poker games. There was another youth who grew up in Ontario with Echanis as a close friend whose career would in later years intertwine with that of Echanis: Charles (Chuck) Sanders.

Echanis was the eldest of a sister and two brothers. If childhood makes the man, much of what Echanis would become was molded in his youth. Certainly two of his outstanding traits—determination and a love of excitement—were already discernible in his young days. Echanis's mother would later recall, "Mike played guard in basketball and competed in track: high jump and long jump and cross-country. He wasn't too large in high school—he probably weighed about one hundred fifty and was about five feet ten, I guess. Not really big, so he didn't go out for football.... He wasn't a fighter in high school. Mike was rarely in fist fights, but he stood up for himself....

General William Walker, early adventurer in Nicaragua and briefly president of that country.

He was an above-average student. All his teachers said he could have applied himself more and done better. But he was enjoying everything every day."

Mike Sullivan, a school friend of Echanis's, remembered, "He wanted adventure. He was always looking for it. But when it came down to it, he often wasn't there when it started.

"Mike had an inferiority complex about being small when he was in high school. He weighed only one hundred forty-four pounds and wasn't very strong. He surrounded himself with big, strong people. He always did that. He always had an entourage of heavyweights. He had an obsession with being tough. He respected Chuck [Sanders] for that, Chuck was tough."

It was a small town and things were boring for the young. On weekends Mike and his friends cruised around and got into mischief. On one occasion they sawed the limbs off the town Christmas tree. Another time they swiped apples and used them as missiles to break windows in the high school building.

Sullivan recalled another incident. "One night—it was winter—we grabbed a couple of cases of empty pop bottles from somebody's garage. We went to the big hill by the high school stadium and chucked the bottles in front of a couple of cars, but the cars were full of cops on their way to police science classes at the high school! It was real cold. We always wore dark clothing, kind of a uniform, you might say. Black-hooded sweatshirt, dark workout pants with black sneakers.

"In fact, when Mike talked to me about a year ago, he said that the foundations for his stalking techniques were learned as a boy. We learned it was sometimes better to hide than run. Anyway, on this occasion we hid down in the field and under the bleachers. Mike and I jumped a big fence and landed near a cop car and ran in front of it. By the time they got out of the car, we ran toward a pile of weeds in a vacant lot. Mike and me were lying there so close, we could see the shine on one cop's shoes. We bit our fingers to keep from laughing and held our breath so the vapor wouldn't show. The cop walked away and we ran the other way."

In his search for excitement, Echanis drove vehicles wildly. He wrecked every car that his father owned. The pranks Echanis and his pals had played became more serious. Sullivan: "We got to making bombs, pipe bombs, mostly, out of black powder. We tested 'em in the hills. One night around 3:00 A.M. we threw a bomb into a parked VW. We doubled back 'cause it didn't go off right away, just in time to see a bright flash and then hear a loud boom. The windows blew out and the door blew off.

"... Then we made a bigger bomb. There was this old lady that lived near school—a real grouch—used to yell at us for cutting across her lawn. Well, we blew up her woodshed."

The police cracked down on the youths, and after that they prudently settled down. Echanis completed high school in 1969 but did not wait to graduate: he joined the army, something he had long wanted to do. Said Mrs. Echanis: "He would have gone to college if not for Vietnam. There was a war on and it was something important to do. What he wanted to do was go to Vietnam and do a job he felt was important."

Echanis completed his basic training at Fort Ord in California, and subsequently airborne school at Fort Benning, Georgia. He joined the Special Forces, and after Benning, he went to Fort Bragg, North Carolina, for Special Forces training. Then it was off to Vietnam with the 75th Rangers. This was to be a short tour: Echanis arrived in Vietnam in March 1970. On May 7 he was riding through An Khe Pass in a truck when his unit was ambushed. Echanis was hit in the foot by an AK–47 round. He returned the fire but was hit three more times, sustaining head, arm, and leg wounds. For fighting with valor, he was awarded a Bronze Star.

Echanis spent most of the following eight months in and out of a San Francisco hospital. His calf was so badly damaged that the army discharged him in December, 1970, and gave him a total disability pension.

Upon leaving the hospital, Echanis weighed a mere one hundred twenty pounds and was a cripple. His inner determination now came into play. Sanders's father, who was a doctor, told Echanis he had to exercise and use his remaining muscles, and this is what he did; he practically had to learn to walk again. He began lifting weights, and this together with the taking of steroids, enabled Echanis to get his weight up to one hundred fifty pounds. Said his mother, "I believe it was [due to] total mind control and discipline that he did as well as he did."

While still a high school student, Echanis—together with Sanders—had studied judo at a gym, and this was the beginning of his lifelong devotion to the martial arts. Once he was back in shape after his injuries, Echanis returned to martial arts.

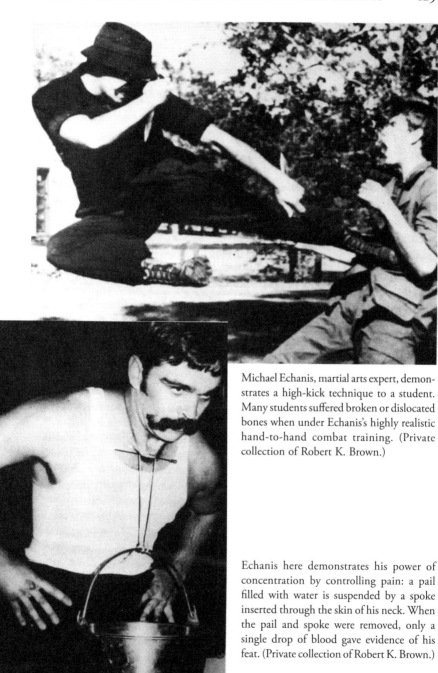

Michael Echanis, martial arts expert, demonstrates a high-kick technique to a student. Many students suffered broken or dislocated bones when under Echanis's highly realistic hand-to-hand combat training. (Private collection of Robert K. Brown.)

Echanis here demonstrates his power of concentration by controlling pain: a pail filled with water is suspended by a spoke inserted through the skin of his neck. When the pail and spoke were removed, only a single drop of blood gave evidence of his feat. (Private collection of Robert K. Brown.)

In another demonstration of his power gained through mental concentration, Echanis held his own in a tug-of-war against twenty-five students. (Private collection of Robert K. Brown.)

Echanis once again demonstrated his prowess as a jeep was driven over his torso without any injury to him. This took place at a SEAL Team–2 reunion in July, 1977, at Little Creek, Virginia, when Mike was meeting with some of the men he had trained in hand-to-hand combat and use of special weapons. (Private collection of Robert K. Brown.)

In 1973 he moved to Boise, Idaho, to study at Jon's Karate–Kung Fu Studio. In 1975, he went to Los Angeles to study under Joo Bang Lee, supreme grand master of hwarang do, a Korean martial art that places as much emphasis on loyalty, courage, and spiritual strength as it does on physical strength and martial art techniques.

Echanis had been interested in *ki* (concentration) power from the time he began to study martial arts. *Ki* helped him to be an excellent student of the arts. After being wounded in Vietnam, Echanis had been in a body cast for a long time, and he was able to use only his brain. He used his healing period to good avail, honing his mental facilities and power to concentrate. Hon Kim, editor of *Black Belt* magazine, stated, "Mike's miraculous recovery after being wounded and his [regained] ability to kick and run were due to his mental ability to control pain and [to] acupuncture performed by Joo Bang Lee." Echanis became so good that he was promoted to *sul sa* (master of infiltration), the first American to achieve this honor. Echanis's concentration became such that he could suspend a thirty-pound bucket of water from a steel spoke pushed through the flesh of his neck.

Echanis built a name for himself in the martial arts field, and his authority was established with his authorship of three books on knife and stick fighting. He developed and set forth a system of combat which *Black Belt* described as the "most effective system of hand-to-hand combat in the modern world" and one of the "deadliest forms of close-quarter combatives ever written." *Soldier of Fortune* magazine stated, "Echanis' systems of survival are an integral part of the background for today's soldier of unconventional warfare."

Echanis went to work for the U.S. Department of Defense, imparting his martial arts skills to the Navy's Seals and the Army's Rangers and Special Forces. He taught armed and unarmed combat techniques. Said Echanis: "In hand-to-hand combat you have but one choice: win or die. Therefore, our training situations attempt to simulate these circumstances as close to reality as possible." In an article Echanis stated:

"… Each individual who expects actually to learn how to defend himself in a life-and-death situation must realize that only endless practice will bring the conditioned reflex, and that the psychological aspects can only be found within the individual during actual combat or the simulation thereof.

"Continual physical and mental preparation is the answer to readiness…. The individual will search within himself to discover, through his own ingenuity and creative ability, techniques that will adapt to the situation and conform to his psychological and physical needs."

Unlike Echanis, Sanders had gone to college. Later he worked as a bartender and bouncer. Following a scrape with the law in Phoenix (suspected of, but never prosecuted for, the armed robbery of two bars), Sanders joined the army. First he went to Officers Candidate School, then switched to the Special Forces. Sanders served four years and won the Soldier's Medal for bravery: he risked his life to save an officer during a dangerous mountain-climbing exercise.

At Fort Bragg, the paths of Mike Echanis and Chuck Sanders crossed again. And it was from Fort Bragg that they were launched into new careers as soldiers of fortune. Echanis came to the attention of Major Anastasio "Tachito" Somoza, son of Nicaragua's president. "Tachito" was taking Special Forces and other courses at Fort Bragg. He was impressed by Echanis and figured he had skills that were sorely needed in Nicaragua. Probably "Tachito" became acquainted with Sanders as well. Echanis and Sanders agreed to go to Nicaragua, and some time around August, 1977, Echanis headed down that way. After Sanders completed his army enlistment tour, he followed about two months later.

In Managua, the two American experts set about training President Somoza's civilian bodyguards. The training was so rugged that a friend of Echanis's recalls, perhaps with a bit of hyperbole, "he put all the bodyguards in the hospital."

In addition to this work, Echanis organized and began training a special detachment of the Nicaraguan National Guard. This unit would range in numbers from thirty to one hundred men. From early in the morning until evening Echanis put the men through rugged paces. They learned close-quarters combat, how to deal with a sniper, how to assault a strongpoint. Although technically only an advisor, Echanis was in fact the *de facto* commander of the detachment. The day would come when he would boast, with good reason, that its men were the equal of any fighting men in the world. The unit was known simply as "Los comandos."

Echanis, serving as Senior Advisor and Head Instructor for advanced hand-to-hand combat for elite U.S. military units, poses here with a wide variety of deadly weapons used in his classes. (Private collection of Robert K. Brown.)

Much of the training that the commandos went through centered on the martial arts, and, of course, specifically on hwarang do. Echanis explained a bit mystically: "Often referred to as the spirit of the warriors, hwarang do is the flowerhood of man—the growth process of life where the experiences of the body, mind and spirit are considered knowledge in themselves. Originally utilized by one of the fiercest fighting sects in Asia, hwarang do methods of training and strict lines of discipline are integrated into the mental and physical development programs of the Nicaraguan commandos, much as they were in the South Korean Division [in Vietnam]."

Author Robert Brown visited Echanis in Nicaragua and later reported: "We drove around in one of the cars that were used by their secret police: an orange carry-all vehicle with no license plates on it.

"Mike and I both had folding-stock FALs with automatic capabilities, and a couple of hand grenades. We felt he was a target; he had mentioned that he was on a hit list. I was concerned. I told him that he was running an exceptionally high profile, but he didn't seem to be concerned.

"He thought he was invincible; there was no one that could get him. But he was easily identifiable wearing a Pancho Villa mustache, plus running around in that orange vehicle.

"Mike was a dedicated anticommunist and he strongly felt that the Somoza regime was the only thing standing between Nicaragua and communism. That's how he justified his position there. He liked money and wanted to be well paid, but he was in no way there solely for money."

On August 22, 1978, a Sandinista commando group wearing military uniforms and pretending to be Somoza's guards burst into the large National Palace in downtown Managua. The building housed two government ministries, other government departments, and both houses of the Nicaraguan congress. The rebels took as hostages the members of congress and thousands of government workers and other persons who were conducting official business there at the time. The Sandinistas demanded the release of political prisoners and a large sum of cash.

Echanis rushed his unit in trucks to the palace. In the sporadic firing underway, the lead truck was hit and one of Echanis's captains was killed. Echanis was eager to attack the building and try to rescue the hostages. He said later: "We wanted to hit them right then, before they got organized, but they [Somoza's military leaders] told us by radio to hold off. We could have taken the building in eighteen minutes. I figured maybe two hundred to three hundred would be killed. The plan was to shock the building with tank fire and blow the doors with recoilless rifles.

"I was going to helicopter in with my commandos and drop down through the roof hatches. The Old Man wouldn't buy it...." The "old man" was Somoza, and he refused to allow the attack for fear of the bloodshed that would result. Instead he gave in to the rebels, letting them leave the country with fifty-nine released prisoners and perhaps $500,000 in cash.

The government's capitulation to the rebel demands did not sit well with officers of the National Guard; Echanis was not alone in having wanted to blast his way into the palace. And what happened at the palace may have had a direct bearing on the final result of Echanis's adventure in Nicaragua.

The peaceful outcome of the palace seizure did not end the country's troubles. Businessmen opposed to Somoza launched a general strike. To support the strike, Sandinistas attacked police and military posts in Managua and other cities. Several interior cities were virtually occupied by rebel forces.

The Guard first concentrated on securing its control in Managua. Then it turned its attention to those cities held by the rebels. Troops supported by rocket-firing aircraft blasted their way into the cities of Masaya, Leon, Chinandega, and Estell. One by one the cities were recaptured. Spearheading the government drive were the commandos of Echanis's detachment. They were playing a historic role in helping the government to suppress a rebellion at least partially communist supported. (Although there were other elements in the revolt that were not communist, the Sandinistas had frequently expressed their Marxist views and clearly accepted support from Cuba.)

To confuse the National Guard the Sandinistas, as they had done at the palace, wore the same standard military uniforms that the guardsmen wore. To resolve the problem of identification, Echanis's men were each issued three differently colored berets. Just before going into battle their officers would tell them which to wear; the opposing Sandinistas would not have time to put on the same headgear.

Echanis himself had seen combat against guerrillas, particularly near the Costa Rican border. (Costa Rica, not having an effective military of its own, was unable to prevent the use of its territory as a Sandinista supply and training area and sanctuary.)

But Echanis did not live to see the victory of the troops he had trained. On September 8 he boarded an Aero Commander with Sanders, a Vietnamese recruited by Echanis named Nguyen "Bobby" Van Nguyen and Brigadier General Jose Ivan Alegrett Perez, operations chief of the Guard. Something happened on the plane during the flight—one report had it that there was an onboard explosion—and it plunged to earth. There were no survivors. The plane had fallen into Lake Nicaragua—the same body of water on which William Walker had launched his own adventure a little over a century and a half earlier.

Did the Aero Commander suffer a mechanical malfunction? Did the Sandinistas succeed in placing an explosive aboard? Or did, perhaps, someone want Alegrett Perez out of the way because of his reported dissatisfaction with what he considered to be the government's "soft policy" at the National Palace? Or were Alegrett and Echanis disposed of because of their loyalty to Somoza? Shortly before he died, Echanis had told a reporter that he had heard about a plot to kill him and Alegrett which aimed at paving the way for the ouster of Somoza by some Guard officers. Said Echanis, "These people were plenty unhappy with the Old Man for his handling of the legislative palace takeover."

Mike Echanis, center and below tower, supervises the training of an elite Nicaraguan commando unit at the Nicaraguan Infantry School in Managua. (Private collection of Robert K. Brown.)

The answer to why Michael Echanis died will probably never be known.

Two of Echanis's books had carried a quotation from John F. Kennedy: "The credit belongs to the man who is actually in the arena, whose face is marred by dirt and sweat and blood ... who knows the great enthusiasm, the great devotions; who spends himself at a worthy cause; who at best knows in the end the triumph of high achievement, and ... if he fails, at least fails daring greatly, so that his place shall never be with those cold, timid souls who know neither victory nor defeat."

With bravery and determination, Mike Echanis had lived and fought the way he desired. A friend would say of Echanis and Sanders: "I think they found in life what they wanted. I think a lot of people go through their lives not finding what they want. They did."

Both men were given military funerals in the United States. In attendance were old buddies from the Special Forces, paying honor to two fighting men for whom the war was now over.

CHAPTER II

John Early: Rhodesian Adventures

Following World War II, the old European empires—English, French, and Portuguese—began breaking up. This dissolution was most apparent in Africa, where more than a score of colonies have become independent nations since 1945. For the first time since European slave traders began seizing blacks for trade, black dominance was established over most of the continent.

Two white enclaves remained, anachronisms of history: in South Africa, a white minority continued in power; and in Rhodesia, a tiny white minority managed barely to hang onto control. Roundly condemned by Britain, the United States, and other countries, Rhodesia was placed in political limbo, under embargo.

Completely outnumbered by blacks within the country and bordering on black countries that bitterly resented continued white rule, the Rhodesian whites fielded a fine army to oppose terrorist organizations but were faced with a serious lack of personnel and qualified officers. To remedy this situation, Rhodesia launched a recruiting program to bring in foreign soldiers of fortune, particularly those who were officer material. Hundreds of Americans responded to the call.

This then, is the story of one of these Americans, and he tells it in his own words.

I was working as a teaching assistant at Southern Illinois University in 1976. I'd been there about three months when a man called and asked, "Are you John Early?" I said, "Yes," and he asked, "Are you recently out of the U.S. Army?" I said "Yes," and asked how he got my phone number, which was unlisted. He said he'd been referred to me by a mutual friend whom he refused to identify. He wanted to see if I was interested in setting up a training operation for a group—he wouldn't tell me where or what it was going to involve. He gave me a California telephone number to call later that evening.

So I called the number and talked to another individual (who did not identify himself) for awhile and he explained roughly what they wanted. They needed someone with experience in training troops, who had actually been trained in setting up companies and battalions, someone with a knowledge of Soviet bloc weapons. When I asked him what weapons we would be using, he mentioned vintage U.S.

weapons—M–1 Garands, M–1 carbines, Thompsons, 3.5 rocket launchers, .30 and .50 caliber machine guns. About a week later, they called me again to see if I was still interested and asked if I'd be willing to come to Chicago to take a polygraph test. I agreed.

Two days later, I received a $200 telegraphic money order for a round-trip plane ticket to Chicago. I flew to Chicago where, as instructed, I went to the Blackstone Hotel and ask for a "Mr. Hutchison." There was nobody there by that name—just an envelope with a piece of paper in it which told me to go to room 1234. I went to the room, where a "Mr. Smith and Mr. Jones" met me with their trusty polygraph. They conducted a routine army-type background investigation. They wouldn't answer any of my questions, hardly talked to me at all. They were friendly and affable, but they definitely didn't want to talk. When it was over, they thanked me, told me to have dinner, stay the night, and catch a plane out the next day.

A few weeks later, I got a phone call from this same person again—I always talked to the same person—and he said I'd been accepted. I would sign a contract in Zaire when I got there, and to show their good faith they were sending me an airline ticket to Kinshasa (Zaire) and $300 expense money. I was told the pay scale started at $1,500 for troopers, $2,000 for NCOs, and $2,500 for officers—captains got $3,000. I was hired as a battalion commander and told I would be given the rank of lieutenant colonel, to be responsible for raising a black battalion staffed by a number of white officers and NCOs. I was supposed to start at $3,500, then renegotiate salary when I was over there.

I really don't know who recruited me. The only person I knew over there was a good friend of mine, a lieutenant by the name of Dennis Wzyareis. Wzyareis has since disappeared. He spoke to me shortly before I went over and said he'd been approached by a government agency; He didn't specify which one, but said he'd been recruited for an operation in Africa and would probably see me in Zaire. The recruitment procedure, however, had followed the lines I had been taught when I was in Special Forces; all the techniques were strictly what I had learned from the intelligence courses in SF. The other unusual thing about it was the polygraph test, which kind of smacked of the CIA or something.

When I got the airline ticket—a one-way ticket to Kinshasa via New York, London, and Luxembourg—I packed my gear and left in early May, 1976.

I arrived during the second week of May, and checked into the Intercontinental Hotel. There were a lot of other foreigners in the hotel, so I milled around for awhile. I met a couple of Brits and saw two other Americans in the hotel.

I talked to one of the Americans for a few hours. He said he was from the FNLA and I asked him when the political representatives would pick us up, and stuff like that. He said he was in the hotel to pick up some people and had picked up about a half dozen or a dozen so far, most of whom looked like Brits—I don't think there were any Americans in the group. When they left the hotel, I looked around the capital and tried to speak to some FNLA political representatives who didn't seem to know what was going on or what I was supposed to be doing. They didn't know what the situation was. They knew I was coming but they didn't have my contract. They said the commander was coming to see me.

Later that evening, I ran into the American again. We sat in the bar and talked for awhile, and he told me he was really discouraged because he wasn't getting any money. Apparently, he had some sort of financial problems at home and needed the money very badly. His general attitude was that the whole deal stunk—not getting paid, not enough medical supplies, no weapons, nobody knowing what they're doing. I generally got a bad taste, and a bad case of nerves, from the whole day.

I still had a little money, so I just bought a plane ticket to Johannesburg. Prior to going there, I had been contacted by the Rhodesian army through a friend of mine who was in it. He told me the Rhodesians were interested in upgrading their airborne tactics and enlarging their school to include a complete free-fall school, so they could get into the HALO (High Altitude Low Opening) parachute business. I went to Johannesburg, then up to Rhodesia, and contacted the people there. I was hired by the Rhodesian air force to expand and modernize the Rhodesian parachute school, which at that time was turning out twenty-four personnel a month—that was their largest class. When I left a year later, we were graduating one hundred and fifty-man classes in the same facilities, with only three additional instructors. We had modernized their training methods and streamlined the school along Fort Benning lines.

At the same time, I was chief airborne advisor to the Commander of Combined Operations, Lieutenant General Peter Walls, and was responsible for training a team of instructors to build a HALO committee. I was responsible for writing the regulations concerning HALO operations and parachute operations in general for the Rhodesian army and air force. It was a commander's dream come true—I could write anything I wanted to. I was writing regulations conforming to what we wanted to do, rather than the other way around. As a result, the Rhodesians have the best airborne capability in Africa, and I would say their airborne capability is quite good even compared to military Western standards.

About a year after the program was set up and running, I was approached by Lieutenant Colonel Ron Reid Daly, commander of the Rhodesian Selous Scouts. I was asked to come run airborne operations and work as executive officer for the out-of-country-strike force. I was to be responsible for planning and executing all airborne operations—specifically, HALO operations for Selous Scouts. So I developed training programs for both black and white personnel and then supervised their training. I was responsible for physically launching the people and recovering them. And in between, two other officers and I were responsible for communications or liaison between the team in the field and the rest of the Rhodesian military. We were

John Early, far left, with a four-man Selous Scouts reconnaissance team deep in Mozambique. (Private collection of John Early.)

like a miniature launch site, except we didn't have any of the facilities you would normally find on a launch site—no reaction force or anything like that.

One thing I did there was set up an airborne delivery system for night resupply of field units with men and supplies. We used a blind drop technique: the aircraft would be given a location and heading to fly. As the aircraft came up on me, I used a Special Forces technique for identification. If the aircraft was on the right heading at the right time, it was my airplane, not a "Fred," the nickname for Mozambique troops, though they did have some civilian planes flying around the area. As the aircraft got closer, I'd talk it in by sound; when I thought he was two to three kilometers away, I instructed the pilot to flash on his navigation lights briefly. I had a QFE altimeter that measures the distance above sea level of the terrain you're on. I'd call the pilot and give him that setting, and he'd set it on his altimeter, so he knew exactly how high above the ground he was. Then I would bring him down to three hundred to four hundred feet on his way in, making sure, of course, there were no obstacles in his way. As he came in, I kept talking him in—left or right, left or right, occasionally having him turn the navigation lights on so I could get an idea of where he was. I'd talk him right in over the top of us and as soon as he came over the top, I'd tell him to start dropping cargo. You can put about 1,100 pounds of equipment out a single door of a C–47 Dakota using the monorail system we designed in three seconds or less, and it won't spread more than two hundred meters at the most.

I brought troops in the same way. Instead of putting lights on the drop zone, I just selected a good drop zone, brought the aircraft in at five hundred feet, and told the pilot when to start dropping people out. We could put twenty-five people with full equipment out of a Dakota at night into an area less than two hundred meters long. We did that by violating just about every rule of safety I'd been taught about dropping equipment and people in the U.S. military. First, we brought the aircraft down to five hundred feet; second, we had the air speed pulled back to seventy knots, so there would be very little forward throw from the plane. And third, all the jumpers were specially trained prior to going in.

I would have all the personnel in the first half of the group steer their parachutes back toward the aircraft as soon as they left the plane. Then the last twelve people, as soon as they checked to see where the twelve people in front of them were, would steer towards them so both ends of the group steered toward each other. The American army, of course, would have had a fit fearing canopy collisions—but military parachutists are trained to take care of canopy collisions. This way everybody would hit the ground in a compact group, and they were off and running in less than ten minutes.

It's an effective technique. and we used it a number of times, without a single casualty. One reason we experienced no casualties resulted from my refusal to allow the people to jump rucksacks. They jumped carrying enough ammunition, water, medical supplies, radio equipment, and rations for two days, contained in a very small pack like the Vietnamese used to carry and rigged like the French carry their equipment. You take the chest straps of the T–10 parachute, hook the shoulder straps of the pack through them, and snap them into the quick ejector box. As soon as you shed your parachute gear, the equipment falls off too. You don't have lowering lines or quickejector hooks to mess with like you do in the American military. You have everything on you. You jump the machine guns with belts in them, though you don't have the weapon cocked. When you hit the ground, you reach up and bust the capewells so you don't get dragged and immediately cock your weapon. You can lie there and fight if you can't get out of the equipment immediately.

We put the troops out with enough equipment to fight and survive for one or two days, and immediately behind them, we would drop their rucksacks and other equipment. If an operation required more than one planeload of personnel, the troops would come in on the first planes, followed by the equipment drop. So, the personnel weren't getting injured on the DZ by carrying a lot of heavy weight, or getting their rucksacks hung up and not lowered in time. At five hundred feet you don't have much time to get a rucksack down—you're in the air less than thirty seconds.

We jumped with reserves as a psychological factor. I had requested permission to jump without reserves—you can't deploy one at five hundred feet—but it was turned down. We had one kid bust a reserve in a door, going out, but his main parachute opened and the reserve just fell down under it. Other than that, no one used them anyway.

I always went in first to check the drop zones to make sure they were exactly what I wanted. I used aerial photos if I could get the air force to fly photo missions. I would usually have to use air photos that were two or three years old. When I found a drop zone, I'd check it for two to three days, and I'd always maintain twenty-four to forty-eight-hour surveillance on a drop zone before I brought anybody in. Then I'd make radio contact with our airborne forces standing by at a launch site, and tell them the date and time to bring them in. It worked fine for us every time.

Normally, in elite units such as Selous Scouts and (Rhodesian) Special Air Service, you'll find captains and majors flying in helicopters overhead, trying to direct the operation rather than being on the ground, leading their men as the operation progresses. I think that's why American officers are well received in Rhodesian combat commands. We're taught to lead by example, to lead from up front. And the NCOs and troops love the major or captain out there in the field humping a pack with them and going through the same thing they are—they'll do anything in the world for them.

For example, I hadn't been in the Scouts very long, and I was working out of Motoko. It was raining like a son-of-a-bitch, and I came into Motoko with some of my people. RLI had just brought one of their fire forces into base by truck. and the troopies were eating cold rations, sitting underneath the trucks to get out of the rain. Not fifty meters away from the trucks was a small tent set up with a floor in it, tables, and chairs, tablecloths, linens and silverware, glasses, and waiters—everything. This was for the corporals and sergeants. About twenty-five meters away from them was the officers' mess tent, set up the same way, just a little larger and more elaborate. The enlisted men were sitting underneath the trucks in the rain, eating cold food, watching these guys being served hot meals by waiters. I was sitting underneath the trucks with one of my men, looking at this. I said, "What is going on?" He replied, "What do you mean, sir?"

"How come there aren't any tents for the troops?"

He said, "The troops don't have tents, sir. The officers and NCOs have their tents but we just put up our own little shelters, or whatever we can." So I went into my lunatic act and stormed into the sergeants' mess, screaming and yelling at a couple of senior sergeants. Rhodesian NCOs are badly intimidated by officers, so I was able to get some shelters put up so my men could at least have hot tea and get out of the rain. There wasn't any chance of getting warm food for them, though. I saw this happen many times.

Early with some of the tank equipment with which the Scouts were so successful. (Private collection of John Early.)

The Rhodesian enlisted men accept the situation because, "It's always been done that way." Whenever they get to be sergeants or corporals, they'll be able to sit in a tent and eat like that and have a batman. But when they're a troopie or a lance corporal, they get the short end of the stick, and they are used to it.

So it caused some rather strange reactions whenever I treated my troops differently. I had a little ritual I conducted before every operation. After all the rehearsals and briefings, when everything was packed and ready to go, about eight hours prior to the launching of the operation, I'd have the cook lay on a steak dinner with all the trimmings and uncork a bottle of wine or two. It had a beneficial psychological effect on the troops. You should always be psychologically up for any operation. My father spent thirty-two years in the army and used to say, "When you go on an operation, you prepare for it. Go into it with the same frame of mind you have when you go out with your best girlfriend. Feel the best you can, look the best you can." He used to advocate haircuts, shined shoes, pressed fatigues—the whole shooting match—whenever you went off on an operation. He said if you looked good, and you felt good, then you'd work well in the field.

The first time I did it, there were four of us. There must have been eight officers watching us—they just couldn't understand what this lunatic from America was doing. The soldiers loved it; though—they talked about that meal for two years.

I don't consider myself a professional soldier. I consider myself a professional combat leader, and I think it's a very important distinction. A professional combat leader does just what the name implies—he leads troops in combat situations. A professional soldier is a man who is in the military for a career but doesn't necessarily spend a great deal of time in combat. There are excellent professional people who do not like to get shot at—I don't know anybody who does, actually—but who do not want to pull combat tours. They are perfectly happy to do adequate or excellent staff work, whereas my staff work is lousy. I couldn't administer a roll of toilet paper.

I don't like getting shot at, but if you want to play the game, there are certain things you just have to put up with. A lot of people like to fish but most of them don't like baiting a hook. It's the same thing being a combat leader—I don't like being shot at, but I don't really think about it. When I'm leading troops, I'm more concerned about the mission to be accomplished—how to maneuver my men and keep them from getting injured or killed, how to coordinate my supporting fires—and obtain my objective—than I am about getting shot at. I just try to block it out of my mind as much as I possibly can. But I stay scared from the minute I go into the field to the minute I come out.

The satisfaction you receive makes it worth it, though. When I'm leading an operation and make contact with the enemy, I know immediately the decisions I make must be correct. They have to be quick, or somebody's going to get hurt. And whenever I'm making those decisions—maneuvering my men, maintaining pressure on the enemy—everything is working right, it's clicking. It's kind of like a ballet and I can see the pressure begin to build up on the enemy, then see him start to disintegrate, see him start to collapse. I start pushing him and usually retreat turns into rout, we carry the day and take the objective. And then, I look around to see what I've accomplished. I see the amount of damage inflicted, and the feeling of self-satisfaction is really great. The sense of accomplishment is immediate. The results of my actions are visible. I've found nothing to correspond with this feeling in civilian life.

I'd say a large number of Americans and foreigners serving in Rhodesia are people escaping from things somewhere else. I think a lot of people turn into mercenaries because they're great escapists—a lot of the marginal ones especially are running from something, or maybe to something. I know a lot of men who left the American or British army and went into the Rhodesian army or mercenary business are looking for some thing, something they experienced once before when they were in the military—a sense of self-worth, a sense of importance and accomplishment, and the camaraderie that develops between people who serve under fire together. There is a bond among men who have risked their lives together. A lot of people are looking for that. I would say the majority of the Americans serving in Rhodesia are looking for that.

The four years I spent in Vietnam were the best four years I ever had. I was important, I had a great deal of self-worth, I accounted for something. I was accomplishing something. It didn't make any difference that what we were doing was either incorrect or badly managed or bungled politically. What we were doing on that spot of ground at that time was important to us. We believed in each other, and we trusted each other. That was a very important consideration. I think a lot of people are looking for that. That's what I looked for.

I am not a very ideologically oriented person. I am a task-oriented person—a technician, and if the job's right, I'll probably take it. I wouldn't work for the communists though. I don't know why and I can't give a satisfactory explanation for that, even to myself. It's a gut feeling, I guess. I've grown up with a concept of "them and us." I've never known a world where we weren't in direct or indirect confrontation with the communists.

During the time I was in Rhodesia, the operations I participated in varied widely, from one-man airborne insertions to large-scale conventional operations. As time went on, I assumed some responsibility for ground vehicle operations in Mozambique as well as the airborne operations. The unit I worked with was commanded by another American, Major John Murphy, a former U.S. Marine Corps captain and Vietnam vet, so we had two Americans in the command structure.

A major cross-border operation took place in early August, 1976 when our sixty-five-man disguised Selous Scout team attacked a terr camp called Pungwe in Manika Province in Mozambique. We killed 1,184 terrorists and only suffered 4 friendly casualties!

Our operational planning was assisted by information obtained from a terrorist who defected. He told us the camp served as a terr brigade headquarters and as a staging area for terrs moving into Rhodesia; that the camp was filling up with terr troops in preparation for a major attack across the border.

The defector also revealed that the terr camp was resupplied weekly by a truck convoy; that the convoy had not yet arrived that week. He provided us with the complete schedule of how the camp operated. The terrs held a daily formation at about 6:00 A.M. where the troops would participate in physical training, receive political indoctrination and work assignments and classes for the day. Finally, he reported that most of the terr small arms were locked in the armory and only issued for training. That meant that the morning formation would be largely unarmed! Our recon team observed the activities of the camp for a day and a half and confirmed the information we obtained from the defector.

When planning the Pungwe raid, we thought there were only five hundred to six hundred terrs in the camp. We were very surprised to find out after the raid that the camp had contained two thousand to three thousand terrs. The reconnaissance team was unable to move all the way around the camp and had consequently underestimated the number of men. We figured that surprise would be in our favor.

Also, our recon team had determined we could call in air strikes on the camp as the terrs had no antiaircraft capability.

The disguised strike force drove into the camp in eight 2½-ton Unimog trucks with .50 caliber machine guns mounted on them, hoping the terrs would think they were there to resupply the convoy. The black Rhodesians and whites in blackface camouflage were dressed in terrorist uniforms, flying Frelimo flags, and carrying a big picture of Robert Mugabe, the terr leader, on the front truck. The trucks were painted in Frelimo colors. They actually drove onto the parade square where about 3,000 terrorists were having their daily morning formation. The ruse was so successful that, as the vehicles approached the edge of the parade square, a large open gravel area about four hundred meters long by three hundred meters wide, and stopped to form into a skirmish line, the terrorists started clapping and giving the black power salute to our men. The terrs approached the trucks, physically touching the vehicles. Then one reached over and grabbed the pants leg of a driver. He pulled it up, saw white skin, and started screaming, "Marungu, Marungu," which means white man.

There was so much noise and chaos, the terrs didn't realize what was going on. Then our men opened up with the .50 caliber machine guns. They literally blew away rank after rank of terrs. As we hoped, most of the terrorists were unarmed at the time—their weapons locked in the armory. One of the .50 caliber gunners said when he opened up on a line of terrs it was like falling dominos. The initial fire fight, if you could call it that, started at 6:30 A.M. and was over in about thirty minutes. By 8:30 A.M. the .50s, which had been allocated five thousand rounds each, were out of ammo. For the next six and a half hours the raiding party shot terrs out of bunkers, trenches, and buildings.

They were also looking for specific terrs. They had brought the defector with them and he identified terr leaders, instructors, etc.… They captured and brought back to Rhodesia the whole damn terr brigade staff—about thirty to forty men. A spinoff of the raid was that the additional intelligence gained from these prisoners assisted the Selous Scouts in planning future cross-border operations. After eliminating all opposition, the Scouts burned all the buildings and the armory, turned around, and simply drove back to Rhodesia.

The Pungwe raid was the first Rhodesian large cross-border operation. That raid made the Scouts a name. And, to date, according to LTG Peter Walls, the Selous Scouts have killed and captured more terrorists than the entire Rhodesian army!

On one occasion we decided to target our efforts against the terrs who were robbing civilian buses. I took a six-month period, graphed all the bus robberies—time of day, location, bus line that was hit, day of the week that the robbery occurred, amount of money taken, and the number of people assaulted, killed, or abducted. The Rhodesians wanted to know why I was graphing it. I said, "Well, if you graph it, a pattern will emerge. People are predictable. They do the same things over and over again, even terrorists. So if you graph it out, you can visually see what they're doing and when."

What we found was quite interesting. There were two bus lines out of eighty being hit consistently. One line was hit one hundred thirty-five times in a month. The next closest was hit only seventeen to eighteen times, and the latter had their buses burned—the former didn't.

We made further inquiries and found out the chap who owned the bus line hit most often was colored—the bus line being burned was owned by a European. The rest of the bus lines were owned by blacks. I checked with the police and found out whenever a bus was robbed, the government compensated the bus company for the amount of money stolen. I became curious: here is a man constantly being robbed, yet still buying more buses and expanding his operation.

So with a couple of friends, I went out to see this guy. We posed as reporters and photographers from a U.S. magazine called *American Modelers*. I said that in the United States there were a lot of people who built model airplanes, model boats and trains, and model buses. And I said we were interested in taking pictures of his buses and learning about his operation, to write an article for this magazine. This guy thought, "This is wonderful! These guys came all the way from the United States to do an article on me and my company." He opened up his entire operation to us.

I needed to obtain the paint color schemes of his vehicles, because I was going to drive down the road in a bus disguised like one of his, to fire up the terrorists the next time they robbed the thing. I didn't want to tip the guy off, but I was suspicious of his operation. I said, "You are getting hit a lot." He replied, "Yeah, we're being robbed all the time, but it's not too bad. I'm doing OK. This is really a great bus line. You should tell people when they come over here for safari, they ought to use my buses, 'cause I've got these brand new ones right here in the warehouse." Then I disguised ten of my African scouts as terrorists and we held up two buses. The bus drivers thought we were a new gang, confessed, and implicated the owner.

So I talked to Special Branch, Rhodesia's combination CIA and FBI, and asked them about this guy. They told me when he was robbed, he received compensation. We determined this guy had made a deal with the terrorists. Also, they were using his buses as a clandestine transportation system to move in the area. They would hold him up periodically, giving the bus driver a cut of the holdup money, kicking back a certain percent to the bus owner, and keeping the rest. The bus line, of course, was being compensated for the whole shooting match. So the guy is making twice the amount of money carrying people just to get robbed. The cops never saw it.

Once we saw what the guy was doing, the police arrested him and he confessed. In the meantime, we had painted his color scheme on our "Q" bus. We'd obtained the bus schedules when we were working in the bus line office. We just went in and looked at his books when he wasn't there—his employees thought we were welcome.

Our bus was armored and totally mine-proofed. It had a little trap door in the floor so you could drop people through it and engage the enemy from beneath the bus. It had fifteen little trap-doors on the side at floor level, all the way down the side of the bus. They could be opened from the inside so you could shoot out.

I took twenty black soldiers with RPDs and MAGs and stuck them in the bus, dressed up as women and kids, put chickens in the thing and suitcases on top. At first we mounted a .50 caliber machine gun on top, but we couldn't get the phony suitcases to flip down so we could engage the terrorists. We had nine 40mm rockets attached to the front grill of the bus in a fan spread, and identical systems on both sides. If you extend all the fingers on your hand, that's what the device looked like. The rocket devices were electronically actuated by the driver. When actuated, the rockets started firing from both sides and the front, one after another.

We found out the typical terr procedure was to have the terr commander stand in the middle of the road with his AK held in the air. When the bus stopped, the terrs would approach the front and both sides of the bus from the bush. The terr detachment commander, security officer, and political commissar would then board the bus and order everybody off. Once all passengers were off, the terrs would take what they wanted, then allow the passengers and bus to continue on their way.

If it was a bus from the United Bus Line, though, which is government owned, or one owned by a white man, they would burn it.

We loaded the bus with twenty people, with twenty machine guns and twenty-seven rockets, and drove around the roads on the bus schedule. We passed a lot of Africans standing by bus stops, so we had one trooper, playing the part of the conductor, standing in the door and saying, "We're full, there's another bus coming along behind us."

We had four dry runs. The fifth run was a near disaster. It had rained and the ground turned to quicksand in spots. The bus hit a soft place and sank in up to its axles.

Here we were with this damn bus in the middle of Tribal Trust Land, with all these weapons on it. We didn't want the Africans to get too close to it, and we were in a real panic. We got on the radio and called up the Rhodesian army reaction force which was about ten kilometers away, held in reserve, to save us if things got bad. They came and pretended to be an army convoy who out of the goodness of their hearts pulled us out of the mud.

The sixth time we drove down the road—at last—there were our terrs, standing in the middle of the road. The bus driver started yelling, "Captain Early, Captain Early, look! There they are, right in the middle of the road." So I told him to take it easy and not get upset. We drove up to this guy and stopped, whereupon the bus driver punched the detonating button for the rockets. They went off and it felt and looked like the whole bus blew up. Everybody inside just held their heads because of the terrific concussion. There was dirt and smoke and all kinds of stuff all over the place—we had never test-fired this thing with anybody inside it. There were twenty stunned people inside, with all these machine guns going—we wondered if we'd hit a land mine! Outside there was nobody in sight, just pieces of people, weapons, and all kinds of things dangling from trees and hanging in the bushes.

The terr detachment commander was lying at a forty-fivedegree angle from the door. He'd started walking around the bus when the thing went off. One of the rockets had caught him in the leg and blown it off. He was in bad shape—he had lost a leg, had shrapnel in the other leg, a couple of chest wounds, shrapnel in the head, and one hand all messed up. But he was the only one in any kind of condition to talk—the rest were dead. We had zapped nineteen terrs! Nobody got away.

We took the detachment commander to the hospital. Two weeks later, we brought him back to the area with the Rhodesian Light Infantry (RLI) and used him to track down the other detachments. They carried him around on a stretcher for a week or so while they hunted down the rest of the gangs in that area. After what had happened to him, it was impossible to shut him up. The RLI eventually ended up getting about forty or fifty terrs out of that area and totally paralyzed the terr organization in that whole Tribal Trust Land.

We had to drive this thing back through the Tribal Trust Land to get back out to the main road. And here was our bus with all the sides buckled and warped and the windows out. This was a one-time operation—we had blown our cover—literally! Everybody was sitting there with their machine guns sticking out the windows, and the people standing by the bus stop watched us go by again. The word goes through a Tribal Trust Land in nothing flat whenever anything strange happens, and I'm sure they probably figured it out real fast. But the rainy season was starting anyway, and the roads got too bad for us to work back in that area anymore.

A few months prior to the bus scene, during one of the ambush operations, we ran across a telecommunication station that was garrisoned by a company of Frelimo. Once we saw how large the installation was, we decided on our own to hit it. We fired a few RPG–7 rounds into the mircrowave screen and messed them up but good. We didn't ambush the technicians sent out to repair the damage. However, a message was conveyed through unofficial diplomatic channels to the U.S. firm providing the technicians that it would not be healthy for them to return. So, the telecommunication system in Mozambique is still pretty well screwed up.

Later we carried out a small raid into Zambia, about forty or fifty miles outside of Lusaka. When we went in, there were only about two hundred terrs in this camp; we took out about one hundred of them. It was a joint SAS/Selous Scouts operation, one of the few times the units operated together. We discovered there were other camps nearer Lusaka that were larger, so they started making plans to take them out. I went back to Salisbury with John Murphy then, since our contracts were just about up—we were due to leave in June—so we didn't have anything to do after that. I assume because they were getting ready to go into the peace talks they were trying to get a ceasefire into effect at the time. Later on though, in August or September, 1978, they went back into the same area—the Zambian camp near Lusaka—and put a major raid in there within about ten kilometers of Lusaka.

The only raid I've ever made into Botswana was an accident. We were allowed the prerogative of hot pursuit. I was working up in the Victoria Falls area on this clandestine thing with the Land Rovers and the bus and the trucks, and I had four of my gun trucks with me. A SAS unit was ambushed on a road about fifteen kilometers from the Rhodesian/Botswana border. I happened to be on my way to Victoria Falls when I heard it on the radio, so we diverted our vehicles and married up with the SAS people. I had my trackers with me, put them on the spoor, called in and got permission to conduct a hot pursuit, and we tracked them across the border to a Botswana police outpost which was known to harbor about one hundred terrorists at all times. The terrs used the police station as a base from which they raided into the Wankie area. We tracked them into the Botswana Defense Force camp and killed twenty-four of them. We nailed two Botswana Defense Force Land Rovers, and I think we killed a couple of their people too, although I'm not sure.

When Murphy and I returned to Salisbury, General Walls took us in and started talking about the settlement they were going to make, to a majority-rule government. One of the eleven conditions Nkomo and Mugabe made for effecting the ceasefire and accepting majority-rule government was that Selous Scouts be totally disbanded, and designated personnel from that unit be brought to trial for war crimes. So you can see the position a foreigner would have had in the unit, especially if the government "went over." There would be no chance of a fair trial because Mugabe had already said. "Yes, we're going to treat the white man fairly—why, we're even going to give Smith a fair trial before we hang him." People are going to be put up against the wall.

General Walls brought us in and said, "This is what we think is going to happen. We'd like you to stay on, if you would like to, but we think you should be apprised of this fact." There was nobody there except John Murphy and myself. I think it was a mark of the regard General Walls had for us that he brought the two of us in and told us personally what he thought was going to happen. I don't know if, the other foreigners were told—I don't think they were.

General Walls told me one of the reasons he thought the terrorists were making these demands was because Selous Scouts alone had killed or captured more enemy than the entire army since the war started. That war's been going since 1969-1970, and Scouts have only been in existence since 1973, and hadn't even done anything really punitive until the last two years—most of the time they were just tracking people. When Walls laid it out for us, we decided, what the hell, let's go on home.

You know, if that hadn't been the case, I would have stayed on a yearly or month-to-month contract with the Scouts, or I might have gone over to SAS. I would have liked to see their organization better up close, and it would have been nice to work with more dependable soldiers. The African soldier in the Scouts, though he is very good, is still not nearly as dependable as the average white soldier is.

I think it's the way they've been acculturated. The African has always been told he's inferior, that he can't do a lot of things, that he must depend on the white man for any sort of intelligent, innovative thought. I think this attitude has been inbred into them until they started to believe it. I think the lower educational standard among the Africans has helped perpetuate this attitude, and the way he is treated in society, also.

CHAPTER 12

American Soldiers of Fortune in History

One of the first American soldiers of fortune was first an important figure in our Revolutionary War: John Paul Jones. Jones's naval exploits during the war of the American colonies against England became legendary and initiated the American naval tradition.

Once independence was won, however, the small American navy was a navy no more. In peacetime, there is little place or use for the heroes of wars. What could the United States do with its chief naval hero when there were no vessels for him to command? It gave him a gold medal and sent him on diplomatic missions to Europe.

To the east, Russia and Turkey were engaged in their second war during that period. The Turks were in control of the estuary of the Dnieper (the estuary was known as the Liman) and a Turkish fleet blocked the river's exit to the Black Sea. Catherine II, empress of Russia, wanted the area cleared of the enemy but the Russian Black Sea fleet was not up to the task. Its officers and crew were a motley collection of serfs, pirates, Volga boatmen, and sailors of fortune from half a dozen or so countries. What was needed was a commander—preferably from a country other than Russia—someone who could shape this crowd into a fighting fleet.

Jones was recommended for the task, and when he was sounded out, he indicated he was amenable. Arrangements were made: Jones went to Russia, was given the rank of rear admiral (higher than the rank he held in America) and was paid about $145 per month (more than he had been paid back home).

Jones met with Catherine and she wrote a friend: "I saw him today. I think he will suit our purpose admirably." As for Jones: "I was entirely captivated," he noted, "and put myself into her hands without making any stipulation for my personal advantage."

Jones had Russian uniforms made for himself (the empress gave him about $1,000 for this) and then left the capital at St. Petersburg for his command. On the north shore of the Liman he found his squadron and boarded his flagship, the *Vladimir*. Later he reconnoitered the area in a small boat.

On June 17, 1788, Jones's fleet engaged the enemy force commanded by the Turkish "lord captain," Hassan el-Ghazi. An initial thrust by Russian vessels was repulsed, and then the Turks attacked Jones's right flank. A change of wind enabled Jones to move five ships of his left wing, bringing the Turks under crossfire. They pulled back, but not before losing two or three vessels.

Ten days later, the Turks sailed forth to do battle again. As historian Samuel Eliot Morison has described the scene, the Turks "were bearing down before the wind, with trumpets braying, cymbals clashing and loud cries to Allah to help them slaughter the unbelievers, drinkers of wine and eaters of swine." The American commander addressed his Russian subordinates in French, telling them, "I see in your eyes the souls of heroes; and we shall all learn together to conquer or die for the country!"

Misfortune struck the Turks before the fleets could engage. Hassan el-Ghazi's sixty-four-gun flagship ran aground. The other Turkish ships anchored in disorder. That evening Jones made a personal reconnaissance of the enemy fleet, rowed by a Cossack sailor named Zaporozhye Ivak. At one point they approached the stern of a large Turkish ship. Over the gilded Turkish insignia Jones boldly scrawled with chalk in French: "To Be Burned. Paul Jones."

The Turkish "lord captain" got his vessel afloat, and the next day the two fleets tangled. Jones was victorious again and the Turkish fleet was driven back to the mouth of the Liman. In two days of fighting the Turks lost fifteen vessels and an estimated three thousand men killed; as well as over sixteen hundred sailors captured. The Russian losses: one frigate, eighteen men killed and sixty-seven wounded. (The Turkish ship which Jones had marked was indeed attacked and burned by the *Vladimir*.)

Jones's victory enabled the Russians to lay down a sea and land siege of the Turkish strongpoint on Ochakov Peninsula at the mouth of the Liman. Jones established a fairly effective naval blockade of Ochakov and was involved in minor actions. Then he fell out, however, with the overall Russian commander, Field Marshal Grigori Potemkin, telling him that "I did not come here as an adventurer or charlatan or to repair a ruined fortune...."

Jones was relieved of his command; he left his flagship November 9, precisely five months to the day after he had raised his flag on it. On December 17 Ochakov was taken by storm—a victory Jones had helped achieve.

Jones was received in St. Petersburg by the empress, and he hoped for a new command. While waiting, he prepared a plan for a commercial alliance between Russia and the United States, and he outlined a plan for the reorganization of Russia's Black Sea fleet. The fleet reorganization was later carried out. John Paul Jones, however, did not receive another command. In fact, he never again commanded a ship or fleet. Soldiers of fortune are appreciated when needed; they are cast aside when victory is won.

They were a tiny band, but no military group has evoked greater visions of fighting romance, and does so even today, more than six decades later. They were the

Americans (and a few Frenchmen) of the Escadrille Lafayette, flying and fighting for France in World War I.

It was August, 1914 and France, glorious France, was at war. Her sons rallied to her cause, and so did thousands of foreigners living in France, offering their services as individuals and as national groups. Among them, the Americans—a group of Yanks trooped into the office of U.S. Ambassador Myron Herrick and asked if it were legal for them to fight for France.

Herrick responded that if they enlisted in the French Army they would lose their American citizenship—that was U.S. law. But, he said, if they joined the French Foreign Legion, the risk of losing their citizenship was slight. Enlistment in the Legion did not entail an oath of allegiance to France; prospective Legionnaires were only required "to serve with faithfulness and honor" and to go with the Legion wherever it might be sent.

The ambassador slammed his fist on his desk and concluded, "That is the law, boys, but if I were young and in your shoes I know mighty well what I would do!" The youths set up a shout, shook hands with the ambassador, and set out on their adventure.

On August 21, in a ceremony in the courtyard of the Hôtel des Invalides, men from more than a dozen countries were accepted into the Légion Etrangère. Among them were forty-three Americans. The pay for these soldiers of "fortune" would be thirty cents a month.

One of the Yanks was an experienced flyer. He was William Thaw II, scion of a wealthy Pittsburgh family who had left Yale to devote his time to flying. He had won fame by being the first man to fly up New York's East River, passing underneath its four bridges.

The Legionnaires were trained and sent into combat. Thaw, however, did not lose his interest in flying. One day he and two other Americans, Bert Hall and James Bach, hiked to a flying field, where they explained that they wanted to transfer to the French air service.

Their transfer to the Service Aéronautique came through, and Hall and Bach were placed in training. Thaw, being an experienced flyer, was made an aerial gunner and then a pilot. Posted to an observation unit, he had the distinction of being the first American pilot to fly against the Germans in the war. His skill in bringing in a plane badly damaged by antiaircraft fire earned him a citation and promotion to sergeant.

A fourth American entered the French air service, and it was his dream that resulted in the formation of the famed Escadrille. He was Norman Prince: son of a wealthy New England family, a Harvard lawyer, fluent in French because of the summers spent in that country—and a licensed pilot. Joining the air service, Prince conducted a campaign, aided by other Americans, to have the French set up a squadron composed of American airmen. The efforts received a considerable boost when wealthy William K. Vanderbilt and his wife provided $20,000 in funds for such a squadron. Vanderbilt favored greater American assistance to the Allies and had already paid for a great deal of medical supplies for them. His assistance to the squadron was to continue after it was formed.

On April 20, 1916, l'Escadrille Américaine was officially established. (Later it would be called l'Escadrille des Volontaires and then finally, l'Escadrille Lafayette.) On the air service's rolls the unit was listed simply as N. 124. Selected to command the squadron of nine was a French flyer, a graduate of the St. Cyr military academy, Captain Georges Thériault. The executive officer was another Frenchman, Lieutenant Alfred de Laage de Meux, who had been serving in an observation squadron. Seven American pilots were assigned to the squadron, including Thaw, Prince, and Hall. (Bach served with another squadron, as did another 142 American pilots of fortune.) Later the Escadrille would pick its insignia: an Indian head.

The Escadrille began its operational role at Luxeuil-Ies-Bains, a small town in northeastern France, where it was assigned to provide escort for a bombardment squadron. On May 13 the squadron staged its first patrol: five of its six new Nieuport aircraft cruised over enemy lines and were fired at by an antiaircraft battery. They flew over a field used by Fokkers and challenged these to a fight, but no Germans came.

In the months ahead, however, the Americans had their fill of combat. The Escadrille was sent to take part in the bitter land and air fighting for Verdun. On May 22, two days after arriving on the scene, the Escadrille drew its first blood when Hall shot down a German Aviatik plane. And two days later Thaw downed a Fokker.

The Escadrille suffered losses, too: pilots wounded, planes damaged and, on June 23, one of the original seven Americans in the Escadrille, Victor E. Chapman, was killed in a dogfight. A Frenchman serving with the Escadrille, G. Raoul Lufbery (a reverse soldier of fortune: he had served for two years in the Philippines with the U.S. Army) succinctly described air combat to a news correspondent:

Lufbery: "I saw a single German machine and I went for him."

Correspondent: "What were your sensations at the moment?"

Lufbery: "Didn't have time for sensations. I began firing at him. Then we both circled, firing all the time. Suddenly, his machine seemed to turn all white. He was upside down. Then he caught fire. He fell, reminding me of a smoking cigarette butt dropping through the air. Then I came home."

After 113 days in the aerial frontlines, the men of the Escadrille were given leave in Paris. By then they had scored thirteen confirmed victories; Chapman was the only comrade who had been killed.

The warriors of the air flew their skies and fought their foes. They did dangerous missions, engaged in dogfights, downed enemy craft—and suffered their losses. Second Lieutenant Prince, founder of the Escadrille, died as a result of injuries received in a landing accident. Lieutenant de Laage, second in command, died in another accident. Second Lieutenant Kiffln Y. Rockwell, also one of the original group, the son of a Confederate soldier, was killed in a dogfight. (Of the original nine members of the Escadrille, five were killed before the end of the war.)

But others came to replace the fallen: men like Edmond Charles Clinton Genêt, great-great-grandson of Citizen Edmond Genêt, who had been sent to the United States to represent France's revolutionary government in 1793; Charles H. Dolan II, an engineer; William E. Dugan Jr., a former banana plantation manager; Henry Sweet Jones, a former ambulance driver; Ray C. Bridgman, lover of literature; and James Norman Hall, who himself would one day become a notable writer.

The entrance of the United States into the war did not terminate the Lafayette Squadron's actions. It was months before American troops saw combat, and American air "power" was minimal. The entire U.S. Air Service had but thirty-five officers who could fly, and General John J. Pershing noted that of these, "with the exception of five or six officers, none of them could have met the requirement of modern battle conditions." It was understandable that the men of the Escadrille preferred to continue flying as a unit under the French flag.

Eventually, however, under pressure to transfer to the American air service, the men agreed to do so provided they could do this as a unit. A few days before Christmas, 1917, the pilots of the Escadrille were formally discharged by the French Aeronautical Service. Due to bureaucratic delays, however, their transfer to the U.S. service was not yet set. The men continued flying for France.

Finally, on January 19, 1918, Thaw was commissioned a major in the U.S. Air Service with orders to command U.S. 103 Pursuit Squadron, which would replace the Lafayette Squadron. On February 18, l'Escadrille Lafayette disappeared as a unit from the Western Front. The legend of l'Escadrille would, however, long live on. It had been an operational unit with the French air service for twenty-two months, less two days. The active rolls of the squadron did not usually go much above twenty pilots at any one time and often were lower than that. The total number of pilots in the Escadrille during its existence: forty-three. Its men had shot down thirty-nine German aircraft (confirmed). Six squadron pilots were killed in air combat, one was killed by antiaircraft fire, and two died in operational accidents. Five flyers were wounded badly enough to require hospitalization.

U.S. Ambassador Herrick stated, "The people of the United States owe a special debt to these boys." A general at French general headquarters said: "When men who have no obligation to fight, who could not possibly be criticized if they did not fight—yet nevertheless decide upon their own individual initiative to risk their lives in defense of a cause they hold dear—then we are in the presence of true heroes. The young Americans who entered the Légion Etrangère and the Escadrille Américaine are in every sense heroes, and France owes them all the homage the word implies."

Mercenaries and soldiers of fortune rarely receive just credit for work done. Even more rarely are they given credit for changing the course of history, but American soldiers of fortune who flew for the Polish air force against Russian invaders in 1920 earned such a place in history.

In 1919, following the Russian Revolution and the exhaustive World War I, the European states were in turmoil. Russian Marxists were still consolidating their hold on Russia, while also trying to spread the revolution by working with Marxists from other countries. During the postwar chaos, the disciplined Marxists spread terror and anarchy, trying to bring down Western European countries. Red Spartacists from the factories were fighting demobilized German troops in the streets of Berlin. French socialists and communists banded together to fight the French government, while Britain's militant trade unions went on strike periodically.

Russian Marxists, flushed with the success of their recent revolution, decided to concentrate their energies on spreading the revolution, using the Red Army to march through Europe. A victorious army would provide the support for the European Marxists to topple their weakened native governments. All that stood in their way was Poland.

Poland had only recently broken out from under 130 years of bondage under Russia, Austro-Hungary, and Germany, and it was struggling for existence. It seemed like a pushover—divisive Marxists were already at work in Poland trying to destroy the new nation from within; Bolsheviks on the borders fought the Polish Army, newly formed with veterans of the occupying Russian, German, and Austrian armies, and some men from Turkey.

In the middle of this explosive situation stepped two idealists, Major Cedric E. Fauntleroy and Captain Merian C. Cooper. Both were U.S. Army Air Service pilots, veterans of action in World War I. Cooper had been working with Herbert Hoover's Relief Commission, where his war skills were much in demand to bring supplies to starving civilians caught up in wartorn areas. He saw firsthand the ills wreaked upon the local populace by those calling themselves Marxist, whose philosophy was based on class hatred and who advocated terrorism as a way of dealing with disliked governments. He quit the relief programs in disgust and offered his services as a pilot and officer to Marshal Jozef Pilsudski, the Polish patriot who was trying to bring order and a government to Poland. After convincing Pilsudski that he wanted to join the fight against Poland's enemy, Russia, he was allowed to go to Paris to find other pilots, resigning from the U.S. military as he did so.

In Paris he met Major Fauntleroy, who became enthusiastic about the project and wanted to join. Having staff experience, Major Fauntleroy was mutually accepted as commander of the proposed force of pilots, while Captain Cooper was appointed operational commander. In a short time, combing the bars popular with air service pilots, they added five men to their burgeoning squadron and departed for Poland. Traveling through wartorn and ravaged Europe disguised as guards on a Red Cross typhus relief train, they arrived in Warsaw in September, 1919. Here they met Pilsudski, an old war-horse who was unconvinced that airplanes had any place in a real war, but he gave them reluctant authorization to form a squadron. They were designated the 7th Squadron, Polish Air Force, and picked up six Polish pilots to round out their numbers. The Americans and Poles were veterans of U.S. air forces, the British Royal Flying Corps, the French Foreign Legion, the French air service, the Imperial Russian AF, Turkish AF, and Austro-Hungarian AF—a true band of soldiers of fortune! After some thought, it was decided to name the squadron the Kościuszko Squadron, after the Polish patriot Tadeusz Kościuszko, who had fought as a general in the American Revolution.

In April, 1920, Pilsudski received word, confirmed by aerial reconnaissance, that the Bolsheviks planned to attack Poland soon in an all-out war designed to destroy Poland and light the flame of revolution throughout Europe. Unknown to Pilsudski, Red Russia's famed Konarmiya, a twenty thousand-man cavalry army led by General Semën M. Budënny, had already received orders to march to spearhead an attack on Poland by the two hundred thousand-strong Red Army.

Pilsudski planned to defeat the larger Red Army by invading the Red-controlled Ukraine, then help the Ukrainians establish an independent democratic republic which would serve as a buffer against Soviet aggression.

Pilsudski launched his preemptive blow and the 7th Squadron, one of twenty PAF squadrons, but comprising almost 10 percent of its strength, flew observation, bombing, and strafing missions in support of the advance. The Russians, disorganized due to Ukrainian defections and revolts against Bolshevik excesses, fell back in confusion, but denied Pilsudski his decisive battle. The Poles quickly marched as far as Kien, where Pilsudski ordered a halt.

The Polish army of less then two hundred thousand men became dangerously extended as it advanced farther into Ukrainian territory. It was weakened by the inevitable garrisoning of men along its supply routes, which were exposed to attack. Predating General George Patton's similar use of air power in World War II some twenty-four years later, the PAF found itself covering the flanks of the advancing army, reporting any Russian movements in the Poles' directions, and bombing and strafing any sizable Bolshevik forces. For the first time, aviation broke up ground attacks before they could hit the army's flanks, while proving that any army in the future without air power would suffer unacceptable casualties.

On May 25 the 7th Squadron pilots sighted Budënny's much vaunted and feared Konarmiya, fresh from its battles with the counter-revolutionary White Army. Its columns were miles long as the self-contained fighting force, forerunner of the powerful American armored divisions of World War II, was able to act as an independent striking force. Buck Crawford, the first pilot to sight the group, dived to the attack, machine guns blazing, wreaking unexpected havoc amongst the leading elements of the Konarmiya and beginning a special relationship between the 7th Squadron and the Konarmiya. The arrival of the Konarmiya signaled the beginning of the Soviet counteroffensive. The Konarmiya was to act as a southern flanking force, tying down or destroying Pilsudski's southern front while maintaining constant coordination with the two hundred thousand men of the main Red Army force to the north.

The minuscule Polish air force, with thirty-one planes on the active roster, of which seven were 7th squadron planes, fought a rear guard as the massive Soviet juggernaut rolled up the overextended Polish forces. Polish and Russian sources both acknowledge that the small air force, acting frequently as the sole Polish rear guard, prevented the Russians from annihilating the Polish force. As two Polish armies fell back on Warsaw in the north and Lvov in the south, Europe began quivering with fear, perceiving for the first time the danger. Bolshevik-sponsored strikes, riots, and revolutions erupted as Moscow-directed communists prepared to smooth the Red Army's triumphal march from the totally defeated Poland through the Western democracies.

But the Poles had one last chance, in front of Warsaw. Budënny received orders to head north, to reestablish contact with the main army and avoid a split between the forces. But Budënny, angry over the constant, annoying havoc the small air force, particularly the American 7th squadron, was delivering to his troops, wanted to destroy their base. Budënny had lost thousands of Konarmiya men to daily strafing attacks, and his much-vaunted army was unable to move during the day. So Budënny refused to go north, saying he had,to wipe out the PAF now operating out of Lvov, before he could move anywhere with relative impunity again.

Disregarding numerous direct orders to join the attack on Warsaw, Budënny slowly pressed farther south, trying to stop the annoying Yank hornets. Pilsudski, aided by excellent aerial reconnaissance, saw his chance and threw his main forces into the gap between the Red armies, rolling up to the northern army, unsupported on its flank due to Budënny's disobedience. Budënny, when he finally saw the danger, was effectively pinned down by the American 7th Squadron, his horse-drawn transport and mounted soldiers unable to move north. He withdrew, harassed and beaten, the Konarmiya ragged and defeated for the first time, later to be surrounded and almost annihilated.

The result was that the course of communism and European history was decisively changed. Communist leadership, appalled at the loss of so easy a victory, held secret meetings and decided to devote most of Russia's energies to internal matters. The policy of spreading the revolution outside of Russian borders with the Red Army, was effectively smashed by the catastrophic defeat of the Red Army at the gates of Warsaw. Budënny returned to Moscow to fight political battles with Northern Front General Mikhail Tukachevsky and his Politburo commissar, Leon Trotsky. Years later, Tukachevsky was tried and shot and an assassin hunted down and murdered Trotsky.

Monuments erected by the greatful Poles to the pilots of the Kościuszko squadron were later destroyed by invading Red Armies during World War II. All references in Central European history books were deleted. But the fact is that Americans, comprising less than 10 percent of the PAF, had flown twice the number of sorties as their Polish counterparts. They lost three out of ten original squadron members, with several more wounded. A total of seventeen Americans served with the force. Captain Cooper, captured by Russians, managed to escape some time after the war was over. The unit was demobilized, its pilots replaced by Poles on May 15, 1921.

A larger group of Americans made a more controversial contribution to a cause in Spain during that country's Civil War, 1936–1938. Spain had been fluctuating between degrees of democracy when King Alfonso XIII decided to speed up the process by abdicating in 1931. For the next five years many factions, from ultraleftist utopian reformers to ultraconservative neofascists, fought for a role in Spain's future.

Two major "fronts" were formed, combining the strengths of the various right-of-center factions in the Nationalist Front and the left-of-center factions in the Popular Front. Elections in 1936 gave the Popular Front the majority of parliamentary seats, but it soon became apparent that the Popular Front leaders, believers in the democratic process, did not really reflect the feelings of their voters, many of whom favored either a "worker's dictatorship" as in the Soviet Union, or total anarchy. The National Front was incensed because the flawed constitution left it with no effective opposition voice in parliament, although it had 44 percent of the vote. Within months of the elections, bands of left-wing radicals seized land and revolted in various provinces, while the government, fearful of alienating part of its support, refused to enforce the laws against the radicals. The right-wingers, in the meantime, were treated to previews of chaos to come, in which they would be the victims of violence wherever the radicals took over.

Political murders and anarchy reigned until General Francisco Franco led part of the Spanish army stationed in colonial Morocco against the Iberian peninsula. The Russian communist government, seeing a chance once again to spread communism, decided to back the Popular Front government, the Republicans, while Nazi Germany and Fascist Italy decided to back Franco's Rebels. The Spanish Civil War was on, in full force.

In meetings of the Politburo and Comintern, Soviet dictator Joseph Stalin and other communist leaders tried to decide how best to aid the Republicans in the fight against the Rebels. Out of those meetings came a suggestion for an International Brigade, an aggregate of idealistic foreigners, pro-communists and antifascists. Out of the party ranks came the faithful, ready to give all for the cause. But the volunteers weren't just communists—also included were thousands of antifascists and many refugees from the Nazi and Black Shirt terror. Eventually, over forty thousand men served in brigades.

The intellectual communities in England and the United States took up the cause of the Republican government, seeing fascism as a more terrifying alternative to the present government. Leftists in the United States and England were deceived by the combination of secrecy and bombastic propaganda coming out of what was viewed then as the Great Social Experiment: the communist government of Russia. The extent of the trials and purges of the mid-1930s were still not known, and visitors to the Soviet Union saw exactly what the communist government wanted them to see.

So many Americans and Englishmen, seeking a cause to live for or a meaningful existence away from the throes of America's Great Depression, saw the fight against fascism as the great crusade of the twentieth century. Of the Americans who flocked to the aid of the Republican government, only perhaps 40 percent were communists.

General W. G. Krivitsky, later revealed to be the Soviet Commander for Military Intelligence in Western Europe, was tasked with forming the volunteers into International Brigades. In keeping with his background, the brigades were organized after the Soviet fashion, with a dual chain of command, involving political officers mixed with equal-ranking military commanders. As in the Russian army in World War II—soon to follow—the dual system of command led to problems, with the political commissar in actual control at some times and the military commander in control at others.

The first Americans to arrive were a group of ninety-six men who landed in Europe from the steamship *Normandie,* traveling incognito as second and third-class passengers. When the organizers of the International Brigades saw them, they were amazed at the amounts of clothing, goods, and money these "working-class" Americans brought with them. At that time, a lower-class American owned more material wealth than the relatively well-to-do bourgeoisie of Europe.

One volunteer was already in Europe: six-foot-two-inch-tall Robert Hale Merriman. Merriman, whose father was a lumber-jack and whose mother was a writer, had attended the University of Nevada, where he studied economics, played football, and was in ROTC. He won a scholarship to study economics in Europe and, when war broke out in Spain, volunteered. He was put to work in late January and early February, as the only man with "military" experience, training the ninety-six Americans, soon joined by another three hundred to four hundred. By unanimous consent they called themselves the Abraham Lincoln Battalion and were made a part of the XV International Brigade, with a battalion of Yugoslavs, one of British, and one of Spanish troops.

After five weeks' training at Villeneuve de la Jarce, the XV Brigade was taken to the trenches at Jaramin on February 16. After a nine thousand-man Rebel attack stalled, the American battalion was sent "over the top," using the discredited tactics of World War I. In two attacks, one on February 23 and one on February 27, the battalion suffered over 320 casualties, with 127 killed. Merriman was among the wounded, but would return to command the battalion and later the XV Brigade.

The Lincoln Battalion was withdrawn to accept and train new replacements, now arriving by the hundreds. By May, 1937, two battalions were formed—the veteran Abraham Lincoln Battalion and a new George Washington Battalion, both with over four hundred Yanks. The Yugoslav and Spanish battalions were transferred to another brigade, leaving the XV as an all-English-speaking unit. With the addition of more arrivals, still another battalion was created. After the battalion's American members deadlocked on whether to call this latter battalion the Patrick Henry or Thomas Paine Battalion, the unit's 30 percent Canadian members suggested compromise: name it the Mackenzie-Papineau Battalion, after two famed Canadians who fought for independence from Britain in the nineteenth century. Called the Mac-Pap Battalion for short, it fought alongside the Lincoln and Washington battalions for the rest the war. (Owing to heavy casualties, the Washington battalion was frequently absorbed by the Lincoln and Mac-Pap battalions, disappearing from the record until the next wave of recruits came over.)

From July through October, 1937, the XV International Brigade fought in all the major campaigns of the Civil War, sustaining heavy casualties but winning fame for its members' enthusiasm and dedication. In November, while retraining new recruits, the XV was incorporated into the Fifth Corps of the Spanish Army. The Yanks, British, and Canadians were now well trained and experienced enough to be considered "Regulars" or professional soldiers, instead of just militia.

In November Franco's Rebels attempted to isolate Republican-held Madrid by driving from their strategic town of Teruel to Valencia. But before the drive was really underway, the Republicans launched a surprise attack out of a snowstorm against Teruel on Christmas Day. Teruel, surrounded by high ground, was difficult to defend, as the XV Brigade found out when it was called in to occupy part of the line on December 31. From December through January, 1938, the Lincoln and Mac-Pap battalions were subjected to intense artillery and ground attacks.

Pulled out the first week of February for a rest, the Lincoln and Mac-Pap battalions on February 15 spearheaded an assault on Rebel communications lines. They displayed precise military skill in which the Lincoln battalion followed the Mac-Pap into combat in line, then swung out to the right in echelon, following with a well-timed flanking maneuver on the enemy position, assaulting twice in disciplined steps to take the objective. Then the English and 24th battalions attacked through their positions to drive a wedge deep into enemy lines, inflicting heavy casualties on the Franco forces.

During the two months' heavy fighting around Teruel, a training base had been established, run by American Major Allen Johnson, veteran of several earlier campaigns. It was preparing over one thousand new recruits—Americans, Canadians, British, and some Spaniards—to fill the gaps caused by casualties. Once again, the Washington Battalion combined with the Lincoln as casualties rose, leading to reports by Franco that he had completely destroyed all three of the American battalions.

In March, 1938, up to one hundred thousand Rebels, including fifty thousand Italian and ten thousand German soldiers and eight hundred airplanes, attacked Teruel, a few miles from the Americans' rest camp. The assault drove through Teruel, on its way to Valencia and the sea, a drive that would eventually split the

Republican-held territory in half and seal the doom of the Republican government. The Lincoln, Mac-Pap, and British battalions, up to strength with over five hundred men per unit, rushed to block the enemy advance. But the Rebel push was too big, and, after finding themselves outflanked every time they occupied positions, the battalions were separated from one another and isolated behind enemy lines. Each unit fragmented into small groups and began a sixty-kilometer fighting breakout, trying to reach hastily constructed Republican defense positions on a river line.

Two Lincoln Battalion machine gun crews, unaware of the general retreat, stayed at a key position, holding up Rebel advances in that sector for eight to twelve hours.

Within days the entire XV Brigade had less than five hundred effectives, but it occupied a small town on an important road juncture and held off tank and artillery assaults for three days and nights, giving the Republican lines time to stabilize. Finally regrouping behind new Republican lines, the Brigade's Americans found they had less than two hundred men in the Lincoln-Washington and Mac-Pap battalions. Major Merriman and most of the staff were captured.

Once again, given a couple of weeks to absorb new replacements, the XV Brigade moved to reoccupy positions on the Republican front. But unbeknownst to them, the Republicans were already defeated on both the Bridgade's flanks. The British battalion advanced in marching order at night directly into an Italian tank park at pointblank and was virtually annihilated. Again, the Lincoln and Mac-Pap battalions were surrounded. They fought their way to Gaudesa early the next day, where an attempt to break through was repelled. The unit broke up and men attempted to exfiltrate singly or in small groups.

Two hundred men chose to occupy a hill dominating all roads leading to important towns. They held up long columns of enemy supplies for a day while Franco's artillery, cavalry, and tanks tried to dislodge them. When darkness fell, the survivors attempted to make their way back to Republican lines.

Upon regrouping in friendly territory, the troops found they had only forty Americans and thirty-five Spaniards left in the entire XV Brigade. One hundred fifty American replacements from hospitals, leave, and training camps were added to the Brigade, but now it became a largely Spanish unit, with the Americans serving as officers and NCO cadres. The unit fought once more in the Ebro River offensive in August, 1938, which was designed to show the world the Republican cause was not yet lost. But on September 22, 1938, the Republicans withdrew all foreign volunteers from the war, hoping to get Franco to withdraw his Italian and German troops.

The cause was lost. Of 2,800 Americans who served in the American battalions, approximately 1,000 were killed, 1,000 were wounded, and 400 to 800 went home unharmed. They returned to an America that one year later was gearing up for war with the Nazis. But these Spanish Civil War survivors found themselves shunned by their own nation, suspect because of the strong Communist Party affiliation of the International Brigades. So when World War II was underway and survivors of the

Lincoln, Washington, and Mac-Pap battalions joined the United States forces, they found themselves inexplicably left behind when their units transferred overseas to fight. All their months of valuable combat experience were lost to the United States.

Just as groups of Americans formed air units to fly and fight for France and Poland before and after the United States entered World War I, a generation later another group of Yanks rallied to the cause of the Republic of China, struggling desperately against an invasion by Imperial Japan.

The story of the "Flying Tigers" is basically the story of Claire Lee Chennault. Chennault was a topnotch U.S. fighter pilot in the period after World War I. Commander of a pursuit squadron in Hawaii and later instructor at an air corps school, he studied pursuit tactics and wrote a textbook, *The Role of Defensive Pursuit.* At a time the air corps had come to believe in the near-invincibility of heavily armed bombers, Chennault was a maverick, arguing that bombers were vulnerable to pursuit planes using correct combat tactics.

Chennault was sold on the belief first developed by an early German ace, Oswald Boelcke, and demonstrated by Manfred von Richtofen and his Flying Circus, that pursuit planes fighting as a team were more effective than planes scrambling in individual dogfights. Chennault put it this way: "The difference between the firepower of two opposing forces, other factors being equal, is the square of the difference of the number of fire units. Thus, two planes, flying as a team, and attacking a single enemy plane, enjoyed odds not of two to one, but of four to one."

The air corps gave Chennault what it considered to be an appropriate steed. He was made leader of an acrobatic group known as the "Three Men on a Flying Trapeze." The purpose was not only to demonstrate skillful flying but also to enable Chennault to prove that fighter craft could direct their combined firepower at a single target through difficult aerial maneuvers. Chennault led the exhibition team from 1932 to 1936. His health, however, was failing, not aided by the hard work schedule he imposed upon himself. And he did not see much of a future for himself in the air corps.

Chennault had been asked, through an ex-air corpsman serving as a flight instructor in China, to recommend additional instructors for that country's air force. Chennault had done so, and then came a letter from Madame Chiang Kai-shek, wife of China's leader, offering Chennault himself a contract to come and inspect China's air force and to make recommendations for its improvement. Chennault accepted and on April 30, 1937, with the rank of lieutenant colonel, he was given retirement for medical reasons (specifically, deafness) from the American air corps.

Chennault was the descendant of a soldier of fortune: one of three Chennault brothers who had answered a call by the Marquis de Lafayette in 1778 for volunteers to fight for the colonial cause. Now Claire Chennault himself became a soldier of fortune. Technically he held the rank of colonel in the Chinese Air Force and the position of advisor to the secretary of the Commission for Aeronautical Affairs, the secretary being Madame Chiang.

Chennault was in the midst of his inspection of the Chinese Air Force when, on the night of July 7, 1937, the Japanese marched over the Marco Polo Bridge and launched a conflict that would eventually expand into World War II in the Pacific. Chennault sent a telegram to Generalissimo Chiang Kai-shek offering his services. He did so, he later explained, for three reasons: "I never run from a fight"; he wanted to give his theories of warfare "an acid test in combat"; and "I was convinced that the Sino-Japanese War would be a prelude to a great Pacific war involving the United States."

Chiang cabled Chennault that his services were "gratefully accepted." Chennault was ordered to direct the combat training of airmen at Nanchang, There he found that "combat training at Nanchang was a positive nightmare. Fighter pilots [who were] supposed to be combat-ready crashed and killed themselves in basic trainers. On a muddy field we'd have as many as five landing crack-ups in a day."

Chennault, with a Chinese and American staff, set about preparing the Chinese air force for war. The training and Chennault's tactics paid off. In a five-day period, a small unit of Chinese pilots shot down fifty-four Japanese bombers during three Japanese raids over Nanking, China's capital.

Chennault's work was not limited to training. He often directed combat operations. He set up an early warning net, using telephone and telegraphic facilities, so that key Chinese cities would know when Japanese bombers were en route. And the old, craggy-faced airman participated in combat himself; he has been credited with singlehandedly downing at least forty enemy aircraft.

The odds, nevertheless, were against Chennault and his airmen. Imperial Japan could pour in unlimited air power; China had neither the men nor the planes to stand up to the Japanese indefinitely. The Chinese air force was virtually destroyed, and Japanese aircraft roamed at will. Between one hundred and one hundred fifty enemy bombers appeared daily over the new capital at Chungking, pounding the city relentlessly.

The Chiangs and Chennault decided that Chennault must go to the United States and seek American planes and pilots. In the fall of 1940 Chennault and a Chinese general, P.T. Mow, flew to Washington. It was not a propitious time; the U.S. government's attention was centered on the conflict in Europe. Chennault made the rounds of officialdom, talked and talked. Finally vital support and a direct line to President Roosevelt were secured in the person of Thomas Corcoran, a member of FDR's brain trust who was involved in the China aspect of the Lend-Lease Program. Chennault convinced Corcoran of the validity of his plan to obtain American volunteers, and Corcoran in turn convinced his boss, the president.

An American Volunteer Group was to be set up, and on April 15, 1941, Roosevelt issued an order authorizing reserve officers and enlisted men to resign from U.S.

military services if they wished to join the AVG. (The AVG would later become famed as the Flying Tigers, a name derived from the fierce designs on the noses of their aircraft.)

On July 10 one hundred ten pilots, about one hundred fifty mechanics, and additional support personnel sailed from San Francisco aboard a Dutch liner and headed for the Far East. The AVG was based in Burma at an airfield outside the city of Toungoo, set amid a jungle about 170 miles from Rangoon. The jungle took its toll: heat, humidity, and insects ensured that living conditions were not the best. Within a month five pilots had quit and gone back to the States. (Pay for pilots was $600 a month; for squadron commanders, $750. Travel expenses were paid, quarters were free, there was thirty days' leave with pay and a $30-per-month food allowance—and a $500 bonus for every Japanese plane destroyed.)

The AVG was in Burma because this British-occupied area was not—at the time—subject to attack from Japanese warplanes. Chennault could train his men without interference from the enemy. Also, the AVG, flying P–40s purchased by the Chinese, would be in a position to defend the Burma Road, a lifeline to China running from Rangoon to Kunming, a Chinese city which was being pounded by Japanese aircraft.

To prepare his men for combat Chennault set up a three-phase program: bomber and other multiengine pilots had to be retrained to fly the single-engine P–40. All flyers attended a lecture course on how to fight Japanese aviators (among the textbooks: captured enemy manuals). And third, the AVG pilots went through a practical course, actual flying, in which Chennault taught them the tactics he wanted them to use. Chennault poured into his men all that he had learned in more than two decades of flying and three years of fighting the Japanese.

On December 8 (in the Far East) the Japanese attacked Pearl Harbor. The war Chennault had long expected had come. The Flying Tigers had begun flying their first patrols on October 24, and then, on December 20, they engaged in their first combat. Chennault had moved the Tigers to Kunming, and on the morning of the twentieth he received a warning from the air raid network that a flight of enemy bombers was heading toward that city. A red signal ball was raised at Kunming airport and the Tigers prepared for combat. Soon a second ball was raised, flares were fired, and twenty-four of Chennault's thirty-four available fighter planes took to the air.

The Tigers intercepted the bombers. There were ten of them, flying in three Vs and not escorted by fighter craft. Attacked by the P–40s, the Japanese fired back but also dumped their bombs and headed back to their territory. Before they could escape, six of the bombers had been shot down. One P–40 ran out of gas and crash-landed but the pilot was safe. Later Chennault called his pilots together and, characteristically, told them: "It was a good job, boys, but not good enough. Next time get them all."

The Japanese had invaded Burma and were driving to capture Rangoon. In the air, the Tigers, again flying from Burmese fields, and their RAF allies staunchly attempted to protect the city against fifty to one hundred fifty bomber raids, the bombers escorted by Japanese fighter planes. The allies could not stem the Japanese onslaught but the Tigers wrote a heroic page, making the Imperial Japanese Air Force pay dearly. The Tigers were not able to put up more than twenty planes at anyone time; sometimes there were only five. In the ten weeks prior to the fall of Rangoon on March 8, 1942, the Tigers chalked up 217 confirmed victories and forty-three probables. Five Flying Tiger pilots were killed, one was taken prisoner, and sixteen P–40s were lost in combat. In addition to defending Rangoon, the Tigers also gave close air support to British troops fighting on the ground.

At one point during the battle for Rangoon, when it appeared that the Tigers might be ordered to China, British Prime Minister Winston Churchill personally appealed to President Roosevelt to ask that they remain in Burma. FDR acceded to the request. After the fall of Rangoon Churchill sent a message to the governor of Burma in which he said: "The victories of these Americans over the rice paddies of Burma are comparable in character, if not in scope, with those won by the RAF over the hop fields of Kent in the Battle of Britain."

As the Japanese advanced, the Flying Tigers pulled back, moving from airfield to airfield but fighting all the way. Their losses mounted in the face of overwhelming odds, and they were largely reduced to conducting aerial guerrilla attacks against the foe. On one occasion, however, they scored a notable blow against the Japanese. Driving north through Burma and toward China, the Japanese army had reached the Salween River. Chennault had his armorers fit bomb racks onto four fighters, converting them into "bombers," and these were sent to blast Japanese troops about to cross the river. The Tigers dropped demolition bombs at the top of a mountain gorge, sending landslides and huge boulders onto the enemy soldiers. They then let fall fragmentation bombs and strafed the enemy. The Tigers staged a series of strikes over four days, and the Japanese drive in this area was brought to a halt.

As had occurred with the Escadrille Lafayette during World War I, the need for the AVG disappeared with the entrance of the United States into the war. On December 30, 1941 the induction of the AVG into the U.S. Army Air Corps was authorized. Chennault favored continuation of the Tigers as an independent unit but bowed to U.S. pressure. On April 9 he was recalled to active U.S. duty with the rank of colonel (shortly afterward he was promoted to brigadier general). And at midnight on July 4 the Flying Tigers, as a soldier-of-fortune unit, went out of existence, absorbed by the U.S. 23rd Fighter Squadron.

In a little less than seven months as a combat unit, the Tigers had destroyed 299 enemy aircraft with another 153 probably destroyed. Thirty-two P–40s were lost in air combat and sixty-one on the ground. Thirteen Tigers were killed by enemy action, ten had died in flying accidents, and three had been captured by the Japanese. The

American Volunteer Group was one of the most effective soldier-of-fortune units in modern times.

The Marquis de Lafayette, Baron von Steuben, Tadeusz Kościuszko, Johann Kalb, Kazimierz Pulaski and other soldiers of fortune came to America and helped the United States to gain its independence. Since then the United States—although foreigners have served in its armed forces—has had no need to rely on foreign military talent. American soldiers of fortune, however, have fought under the colors of many countries during the past two centuries. Americans are fighting in Africa and Central America today. And in tomorrow's wars, too, there will be Americans who will take gun in hand and go forth to fight for cause, for money, or for adventure. Some will be unknown and unremembered. But the chances are that there will be future Mickey Marcuses, William Morgans, and Alan Seegers.

In the annals of fighting men, the soldier of fortune is unique.

Index